Broadband Networking ABCs for Managers

ATM, BISDN, Cell/Frame Relay to SONET

Broadband Networking ABCs for Managers

ATM, BISDN, Cell/Frame Relay to SONET

Robert P. Davidson

A Wiley–QED Publication

John Wiley & Sons, Inc.

New York • Chichester • Brisbane • Toronto • Singapore

ISBN 0 471-61954-X

Printed in the United States of America

10 9 8 7 6 5 4 3 2

Contents

Preface

The rapid advancement in communications technology continues to change society for the better. The globalization of economies, the tying together of personal computers into powerful computing facilities, and the sending of mail in the form of facsimile, are all being done over the public telephone network. To meet these needs, the network continuously adapts to the ongoing conversion of information to digital electronic signals capable of being transported over telephone lines. It is estimated that today 97% of our information is on paper or microfilm, so the transference to digital data has just begun.

The onslaught of multimedia information—voice, video, and image—has already transformed the majority of public network traffic from voice to data. The downsizing of information systems has created an equally turbulent growth in local area networks (LANs). LANs were often created with no central planning, and addressed only departmental issues. Today, these once–separate islands of computers are internetworked to such a degree that it is difficult to tell where the LAN ends and the wide area network (WAN) begins. A host of new communication technologies such as voice processing, cell and frame relay, asynchronous transfer mode (ATM) and synchronous optical network (SONET) are encouraging the widespread use of new 'killer' applications. These include mobile computing, image processing, video conferencing, executive information systems, groupware, client/server databases, and voice mail, among others. The broadband networks and services emerging to support these applications—switched multimegabit data service (SMDS), broadband integrated services data network (BISDN), ATM, fiber distributed data interface (FDDI), fast Ethernet, etc.—are all based upon the ubiquitous fiber cable. Knowing how to use these new technologies and services as well as expanding the bandwidth of both private and public networks has become crucial to competitive enterprise.

In global business, the fittest survive. The mainframe has fallen prey to the personal computer, the proprietary computer network to the LAN, and now private corporate networks to integrated public network services. The need is for nothing less than desktop-to-desktop conductivity. Today's commerce demands the real-time transmittal of information to individuals as well as corporations—when, where and in whatever forms are needed. Information once available only to the power broker is now democratized. The need to collect, manage, and use globally available information has never been greater. In today's information–intensive industries, it is the ability to grasp knowledge quickly that provides the competitive edge. Few can afford to ignore this trend because the need to innovate in industries continues to rise, seemingly without end. Companies that adapt to this new information age will prosper because their ability to collect and manage information in real-time will spell the difference between success and failure.

Training is the most important tool. This revolution in digital communications is ongoing, and a whole new generation of network technologies will be combined in various ways to replace traditional public and private networks, computers, telephones and televisions. Managers often lack adequate background for the advanced networks of computers that have become vital to daily business. Often they must plunge into the job without adequate time for training. Worse, the underlying technological premise is changing so rapidly that even specialists have trouble keeping up. In a few short years, decades of voice dominance in the public telephone network have given way to data, copper wire to fiber, and the separation between computers and their networks has blurred.

This book is an attempt to provide the necessary foundation for the understanding of broadband networks. It details the latest fundamental changes taking place in broadband communications with regard to technology and business orientation, and explores the numerous factors driving the development and deployment of broadband networks (Figure P.1). It is thus immediately relevant to networks that are being deployed now.

Chapter 1 describes the new business applications that are changing the workplace. Databases, word processing and spreadsheets that

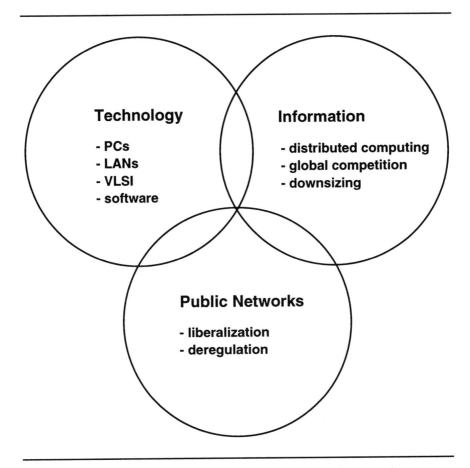

Figure P.1. Broadband network drivers.

were once reserved for individuals are now within the purview of the group, greatly increasing the productivity of all. Global communications networks have removed distance as a criterion for effective contact between people, businesses, and nations. The ability to communicate anywhere, anytime over the public telephone network has become crucial for modern commerce.

Chapter 2 details the communications trends that are accelerating the introduction of broadband networks. In the past decade, data has supplanted voice as the predominant source of public network traffic.

There is no single reason for this. Certainly the global competitive environment, where businesses must be well–informed and nimble to survive, has fueled the flame. Increased numbers of personal computers and sophisticated software applications that make businesses more efficient and effective further contribute because pockets of information must be interconnected. Workgroups share knowledge in the form of images and video as well as text. Entire companies automatically spawn messages into the network to track customers, create conferences for collaborative problem–solving, and access a library of policies, documentation and news. This torrent of demands deluges public and private networks, pressing for intelligent and concurrently managed information superhighways.

Chapter 3 discusses new network applications such as facsimile, E-mail, imaging, groupware, and multimedia, as well as the way that societal and economic pressures will continue to drive the computer and telecommunications industries in the same direction. Trends expanding the home work force (telecommuting) and legislative initiatives promoting the use of the telecommunications network are already creating unrivaled opportunities for broadband technologies and services. But getting from here to there means that customers must understand their options for LANs as well as WANs, and providers must understand the market dynamics. The companies—the broadband data network consumers—that prosper in the 1990s will be the ones who solicit the combinations of features and services uniquely appropriate to their businesses. The vendors that prosper will be those who offer these combinations.

Chapter 4 describes how an early form of broadband network, the LAN, has emerged as the dominant computing environment, replacing earlier mainframe and minicomputer networks. The sharing of information and equipment gives LANs great economy, allowing them to have emerged from the backwaters to the forefront of networking. But it is becoming less likely for users to be concerned only with their immediate environment. Today, users want to communicate and share resources and information, independent of geographic constraints. This encourages the development of better interfaces between LANs and WANs, as well as higher data rates.

Chapter 5 is concerned with the networking elements that LAN internetworks employ. Some networking elements such as the bridge, hub, and repeater have evolved from intra-LAN applications. Others, like the router and gateway, were specifically intended for internetworks. All are evolving toward increasing function and performance. This has led to a new hierarchy in WANs that allows the LAN to extend beyond *its* traditional boundaries. An extended LAN may encompass a city or a metropolis, and have global interconnectivity via the public telephone network.

Chapter 6 describes the broadband technologies that are impacting business productivity. One such technology, *fast packet*, is already a success in private T1 networks. New broadband technologies such as frame and cell relay, SONET and SDH (the synchronous digital hierarchy, SONET'S European equivalent), as well as ATM, have entered the telephone company/post, telephone, and telegraph authority (Telco/ PTT) networks. ATM, for example, allows the Telco/PTT to tailor a variety of services to the specific needs of business and residential customers. Now the same technologies, honed in the WAN, are returning to the LAN mainstream, routing and switching information at unprecedented speeds.

Chapter 7 describes how the present asynchronous telephone network is becoming synchronous. Within the public telephone network there is a hierarchy of rates that go beyond it, referred to as the *asynchronous standard hierarchy*. While consistent at each level, it has little overlap, so asynchronous DS1 frames have little resemblance to DS3 frames. As a result, the public network is synchronous only on a piecemeal basis, and therefore lacks the management capability and bandwidth flexibility for many of the newly demanded services. In contrast, LANs provide inexpensive connectivity at least in a local area. But LANs, too, have come under pressure from the increasing bandwidth demands of new applications. Because of its capacity to manage large amounts of bandwidth, and its simplicity and cost–effectiveness, SONET will, in a few years, totally displace the existing installed base of nonstandard fiber and electronic equipment. Since SONET is a transport technology, it does not necessarily displace emerging technologies such as frame relay, SMDS, FDDI, BISDN and ATM, which can and will be carried by the SONET network.

Chapter 8 continues to detail SONET/SDH networks, concentrating on the new variety of network elements (NEs). Unique features such as direct multiplexing and grooming of DS0s, add/drop capabilities, and the standard optical interfaces will simplify the design and management of broadband networks. SONET equipment will form the tributaries, interoffice trunks, metropolitan and suburban backbones of public and private broadband networks. But there remains a considerable investment in embedded asynchronous equipment; the telephone companies have been slow to replace perfectly usable equipment. The North American and European asynchronous transmission rates fall below those of their SONET counterparts. Although SONET NEs support the major existing framing formats, the reverse is not true. It is not possible to cram SONET signals into the existing network. Pressure from private networks will act as a catalyst to SONET deployment. Within the confines of the corporation, the seeds of SONET will sprout.

Chapter 9 describes the types of broadband networks presently being implemented. One result of their rapid deployment is the bewildering array of new carrier services that seamlessly internetwork LANs and WANs, satisfying the demand for sophisticated data, image, and video communications. Emerging services include switched multimegabit data service (SMDS) offered by the Telco/PTT and BISDN/ATM offered by LAN equipment vendors and Telcos/PTTs. They are dependent upon newly emerging technologies. SONET/SDH forms the basis for linking high-speed LANs, while ATM realizes the full potential of bandwidth-on-demand services. Together they integrate LAN and WAN network elements, using common equipment and making possible a rich variety of network architectures.

Chapter 10 discusses how to plan to make optimum use of the economies and efficiencies afforded by broadband networks—LAN or WAN. The fundamental changes taking place in telecommunications with regard to technology and business orientation are creating new business realities. No business is an island—all are interconnected by a vast global communications network. How effectively the network is used will be determined by how aware network and information management employees are of their new role. This awareness may very well determine a given enterprise's competitive posture.

The explanations within this book are intended to be clear and concise. Unnecessary detail is avoided so what is important can be concentrated upon. How well this goal is met depends upon how valuable you feel after reading it. I welcome your comments.

I also wish to thank my lovely wife Myrna, and my sons Alan, Brian, and Kevin for their support and patience.

—Robert P. Davidson, Ph.D.

1

Introduction

Global communications networks have removed distance as a criterion for effective contact between people, businesses, and nations. Advances in lasers and fiber optics have lead to very high-speed networks that can transmit the contents of a complete encyclopedia in the blink of an eye. In this era of global, multi-enterprise networking, the ability to employ such high-speed technology within the public telephone network has become crucial for modern commerce. Electronic transmission of facsimile, E-mail and EDI among other forms of electronic information has altered the very nature of trade. In today's knowledge-based industries, the rate at which individuals and organizations acquire knowledge is and will remain a significant advantage.

The growth of private corporate networks has slowed and been replaced by an interest in more efficient interconnection with the public network. Yet the existing asynchronous public network infrastructure lacks the bandwidth and intelligence demanded by new applications. These applications combine bandwidth–gobbling, software–based technologies that simplify the interface between the individual and the information, vastly increasing productivity. Moreover, the customer is concerned with desktop-to-desktop transmission, switching, and management that requires a coalescing of public and private network technologies and interfaces. So public networks—at a huge investment cost—must migrate to new, more powerful infrastructures capable of supporting the bandwidth and processing demands of new applications.

The goal of this migration is to create a global network so powerful that it will transform the way we do business, socialize, and play. It will empower the corporate mainframe, the road warrior laptop, allowing them to connect to remote branches, trading partners and customers as well as within an enterprise. They will send and receive telephone calls and mail over terrestrial fiber, satellite, and radio waves without being aware of the route that the information traversed. They will not be limited by place, time, equipment, or media.

This unified, global network will meet information needs on any scale, configuration and application. On command, it will distribute communications between different types of computers and local networks. From the palmtop to the mainframe, from New York to Tokyo, this coupling of people and resources will encourage faster and better decisions, improving profitability and competitiveness. For the first time in history, information will be within the reach of all the people who need it.

This rosy future is not a wide-eyed dream, but will be the result of a natural evolution based on the driving technologies of fiber optics and silicon integrated circuits. Already, fiber optics has lowered network noise levels by orders of magnitude, allowing a multitude of new streamlined communications protocols. And the ubiquitous silicon integrated circuit continues to double in density every nine months. The complexities of the systems that can be constructed in silicon are now powering the communications industry in the same fashion that they once powered the computer industry. The same integrated circuit revolution that made computers more affordable is now fueling broadband LANs and WANs, providing network elements that operate at ultrahigh data rates.

While integrated broadband services will be the driving force in next-generation networking, broadband transport is not a new technology. It has been deployed for decades in the form of public asynchronous backbone networks and private LANs. What is new is the confluence of technologies that allow widespread broadband transmissions over the telephone network. The underlying structure of the public network has changed, with fiber optic cable replacing copper lines. Fiber optic transmission between switching exchanges has become the rule in the industrialized world; its efficiencies, performance and economies have created a multibillion dollar equipment market that is growing at double digits. Less-noisy fiber routes allow information to be transported without the time delays incurred with in-route error checking protocols. Businesses now have at their disposal unprecedented computer power at reasonable prices, increasingly available fiber media, and advances in silicon integrated circuits. In turn, this has allowed the practical implementation of new protocols, interfaces, and switches. These are based on emerging broadband technologies such as SONET, SDH, and ATM.

Taken together, these enabling technologies will allow the WAN to become an extended-distance LAN.

The need for this infrastructure is not springing from the minds of technocrats, but from the traffic generated by everyday industry. Companies willing to install broadband networks will reap the benefits. Network managers must prepare by understanding the trade-offs between, and the motivations for, broadband networks. The largest hurdle is not technological, but the will and ability of companies to train employees and customers, retarget development projects, and pry funds loose to improve the network infrastructure.

1.1. NETWORK TRENDS

In the past, WANs based upon technologies capable of transporting information at T1 or lower rates (less than 1.544 Mb/s) provided adequate transport. These networks were dominated by voice or point-to-point data and packet-switched facilities that connected dispersed business locations and computer equipment. Their architectures supported the access of remote terminals by mainframe or minicomputers. The host-centric networks of the 1980s have given way to distributed computing environments. High-capacity token ring and Ethernet LANs deliver data between desktop workstations and personal computers. Originally, the interconnection of these LANs was limited to building-wide or campus networks, but as communications went global, LAN internets began to deliver the data to the worldwide communication network, exposing weaknesses in the existing broadband network infrastructure. WAN bottlenecks were created and have caused outages, overloads, and intolerable delays for real-time applications, and a glaring lack of bandwidth management.

Businesses previously concerned with their mainframe computer networks are discovering that the WAN is as much a part of their day to day activities as the LAN. It is difficult for them to ignore the changing telecommunications environment—an environment fraught with terminology, protocols and economics different from the more familiar LAN—and remain competitive. Moreover, telecommunication is undergoing change as profound as that imposed upon the mainframe computer by the personal computer. Broadband technology is becoming the key to the future of public and private networks around the world.

1.2. ENTER BROADBAND APPLICATIONS

Broadband networks have the capacity to channel the daily flood of information from local and campus environments and distribute it to remote desktops and information processing resources (Figure 1.1). As the amount of data builds up, it enters broadband channels employing communications speeds beyond T1 rates (1.544 Mb/s). The resulting transmissions may remain within a campus or building, be dispersed through a metropolis, or span the globe. The source of information is not important. What is important is the capacity and routing capability of the networks. Broadband networks are already changing the rules of how business is done with throughput approaching the speed of light. In a world economy where real-time and managed access to massive amounts of information is important, these networks have become vital information superhighways.

The immediate requirement for broadband networks stems from the day to day use of an expanding variety of software programs used in the office environment. The backlog of seemingly simple applications is spawning larger and larger data fields. To remain competitive, leading edge executives need access to current information without geographical or time constraints. They now rely more and more on graphs, pic-

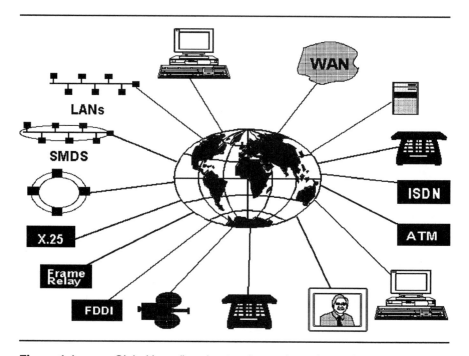

Figure 1.1.   Global broadband networks service voice and data.

tures, tables, and even video with text. As a result, the size of the files used to store information has increased tenfold. This growth has created massive operating systems for personal computers: while the original DOS loaded in two diskettes, Windows requires seven, and OS/2 uses even more. The programs running under these operating systems are already available in multimedia formats that contain multiple graphs, charts, pictures, and text. The commonplace word processor has become more powerful, incorporating capabilities once reserved for spreadsheets, databases and desktop publishers. Several years ago a large spread sheet was 300 kilobytes. Today's financial spreadsheet files contain dozens of graphs that are all updated in real-time and consume from 1.5 to 3 megabytes of memory. Databases and desktop publishers consume even larger amounts of memory.

Transmitting files generated by these programs can be a lengthy process unless enough bandwidth is employed. Telephone companies charge for the amount of bandwidth consumed. Bandwidth determines how quickly information may be transmitted from one point to another in a network. A computer file sent over a 2400 baud bandwidth line takes roughly one hour per megabyte of information. Sending megabytes of data faster demands networks with the capability to supply and route larger bandwidths.

1.3. CONCLUSION

New business applications are permeating the workplace. Databases, word processing, and spreadsheets once reserved for individuals are now within the purview of groups. Global data networks communicate their contents to people, machines, businesses, and nations. The ability to be networked and thus to communicate anywhere, anytime has become crucial for modern commerce. Today's computer and telephone will coalesce and evolve into a completely portable and self-contained communications appliance, going beyond today's pocket electronics. This small hand-held console of the future will instantaneously link a person to any print or visual media in the world over the public telephone network. The basic ingredients for this new way to communicate information are already being deployed—the downsizing personal computer, miniature video displays, and synchronous optical networks. With advanced integrated circuits, digital electronics, and data streams, the real-time packaging and transmittal of information over broadband networks will generate unbelievable gains in business productivity.

2

Communications Trends

2.1. INTRODUCTION

Once limited to voice and low-speed data transport, the communications network is adjusting to the accelerated introduction of data. In the past decade, data has supplanted voice as the predominant source of public network traffic. Hospitals transmit X-ray images to specialists hundreds of miles away, students tap into distant research libraries, and executives log onto office networks from home. Today, these are the exception rather than the rule. For this trend to become even more widespread, a new global network infrastructure is needed in which, for the first time, standardized protocols can flow over a single switching and multiplexing fabric, allowing the internetworking of all types of data communications equipment. All points in the network—public or private, LAN or WAN—will use common technology.

2.2. OPEN SYSTEMS INTERCONNECT (OSI)

The first step in implementing such networks is to adhere to a common model for networking. Earlier proprietary networks such as IBM's systems network architecture (SNA) required equipment from a single vendor. While the network worked fine, it did not allow the customer to use the latest technologies and equipment from other vendors. Nonetheless, IBM's SNA was used as the basis for modeling an open system.

An open system is a network formed by building blocks that adhere to standard protocols.

The foundation for open systems is the Open Systems Interconnect (OSI) reference model (Table 2.1). This model of a communication system, developed by the International Standards Organization (ISO), is most valuable as a way to characterize networks and as a goal for uniform network implementation. Today, all major networking players attempt to characterize their equipment using the model. The model describes the seven steps, or layers, required for end-to-end communications. Each layer communicates with the layer directly above and below, and has its own communications mechanism. This structure allows error checking and recovery at the lowest possible layer, improv-

Table 2.1.   OSI reference model.

7	Application	Uses messages— Communications interface between users and applications, i.e., allows file copying, virtual terminals, etc.
6	Presentation	Transforms data between systems; also may provide decompression and de-encryption.
5	Session	Uses remote procedure calls (RPCs)— Manages dialog between systems; provides remote software functions on the remote system, i.e., no disk space, paper out, etc.
4	Transport	Uses segments— Ensures the reliable delivery of data, usually through connection makes and breaks, acknowledgment messages, sequence numbers, and flow control.
3	Network	Uses datagrams— Provides for data movement across different network segments, organizing the Data Link layer and often including the logical source and destination addresses.
2	Data Link	Uses frames— Organizes the Physical layer in logical groupings, often including the physical source and destination addresses; provides flow control and error detection (sometimes error correction).
1	Physical	Uses bits— Defines the mechanical and electrical requirements of the media and interface hardware.

ing throughput. Most communications systems do not use all of the layers; in fact, the network portion of end-to-end communications is found in layers four and below. Higher layers such as application, presentation, and session are normally associated with the sending or receiving computer. Also associated with the layers is equipment that allows networks to be interconnected—gateways, routers, bridges, and repeaters. Throughout this book, the OSI reference model will be used to describe networks and the equipment that forms them.

2.3.   CLIENT/SERVER COMPUTING

For business, survival may depend on the ability to reduce the time it takes to gather and process information from days to minutes, from hours to seconds. A wide range of industries send and receive information over globally dispersed telephone networks that were originally designed for voice transmission. These businesses are pursuing more efficient ways to swap text and digitized images as they discover that data networking provides needed productivity enhancements. Productivity begins with the LAN.

LANs share computer equipment and information, helping reduce paperwork and enhance intra-office communication. Early LANs employed peer-to-peer networking between two equal devices. This was in stark contrast to the rigid network hierarchy used by mainframe and minicomputer computer networks such as IBM's SNA or DEC's DECnet. Although it freed individuals and small workgroups from unnecessary constraints, peer-to-peer networking was unwieldy for larger networks where security was a concern and more complex applications the rule. In the 1980s, a more powerful LAN architecture evolved called client/server computing. The idea behind client/server computing is to separate the application from the service and then provide a simple path between the two. Such a concept, when put into practice, ensures that the service overhead is only incurred when the service is used. Since each interface in each service remains constant, new applications can be developed anytime. A client/server environment also allows services to be upgraded more easily. Client/server networks include one main microcomputer called the server. The desktop microcomputers are called clients. Ordinarily, all programs that the clients run are located on the server.

There are many client/server applications: on the factory floor, the computer supervising the work flow and a robotic arm controller can use different applications to draw only what each needs from a generic database server. In another case, the shared service could be printing,

E-mail, computer-aided design (CAD) services, and other functions. A client/server computing environment can consolidate a factory's information system (IS) to share hardware, software and data, and ultimately to help reduce any redundancies. Client/server systems can also improve efficiency by distributing processing chores. This is most apparent in engineering departments. For example, one powerful shared workstation can be used as a CAD server to perform finite-element analysis—a computation-intensive task. Meanwhile, engineers can work on a variety of other tasks with less powerful computers. Despite the advantages of client/server computing, it can have drawbacks if one does not pay attention to broadband network details.

2.3.1. Bottlenecks

Often, more time and money is spent worrying about raw connectivity and how to migrate to client/server computing than whether the network will be fast enough to handle client/server traffic. Client/server computing requires faster networks for several reasons (Table 2.2):

* The distributed network increases the network loading, and the physical layout can slow traffic as it passes from bridge to router to gateway.
* There is much more dialog between clients and servers than among machines in traditional host-to-terminal architectures. Important to the exchange is a two-phase commit process, which synchronizes and updates both the receiving and sending databases. For example, a shipping order is guaranteed on both the sending and receiving ends

Table 2.2.   Client/Server network burden.

Activity	Net effect
two-phase commit and distributed network functions	up network traffic 5% to 40%
security checking	increases network overhead 10%; creates five– to 10–second delays
distributed physical layout (hodgepodge of software, hardware and connectivity devices)	hikes transaction volume 2% to 5%

of the transaction. Although the two-phase process ensures database accuracy, it adds significant traffic. Network traffic can rise from five to forty percent depending on the distributed database complexity.

- Sufficient bandwidth is also important for handling failures and peak loads. Distributed networks can use alternate routes on path failure, providing there is bandwidth available. If the network fails and adequate spare bandwidth for rerouting the traffic is lacking, clients can continue to work on the distributed database, but the transactions will not be posted on the server database. In this case, when the path comes back up, updates flood the network, causing congestion.
- Security checking between the client and server also slows transaction time and increases traffic. Clients and servers pass information about users on the network to ensure that client machines are legitimate and not hackers.
- Backup and recovery are also a burden on the network. During backup, large bursts of data hit the network, resulting in a reduction of available bandwidth.

Unless these constraints are recognized and adequate bandwidth provided, the client/server can be a big step backwards. One furniture manufacturer discovered that its client/server network slowed data traffic to such an extent that in six months of poor network performance the company lost nearly $2 million in business and at least $700,000 in employee productivity. This blind application of an advanced technology resulted in the early retirement of the responsible information systems manager. Unfortunately, this is not the only case in which a lack of understanding of network capacity *and the impact desktop intelligence has upon it* has proven disastrous.

2.3.2. Desktop Intelligence

The intelligence of desktop devices has increased dramatically (Figure 2.1). Over the past decade, the cost per millions of instructions per second (MIPS) for computers has declined at an annual rate of 25% per year. The cost per bit for random access memory (RAM) declined at 30% per year, and that of magnetic memory used in disk drives at 25% per year. As a result, mainframe costs have dropped at 15% per year, minicomputers at 25% per year, and personal computers at 31% per year. Yet their power and speed have increased by orders of magnitude. Advances in silicon have made faster microprocessors possible, allowing

	ENIAC	IBM system 370 Model 168	IBM PS/2 Model 70	Dell 486P50
Date	1946	1975	1988	1992
Size	30 tons, about the size of a boxcar	refrigerator size	desktop size	desktop size
Instructions processed per second	100,000	2 million	5 million	19.4 million
Cost	$3,223,846	$8,828,625	$13,840	$2,188

Today's desktop PC is nearly 200 times more powerful than the 30-ton ENIAC, the world's first computer. And progress hasn't stopped: Dell's 486P50 is four times as powerful as a high-powered model IBM sold in 1988, and one-sixth the cost.

Figure 2.1. PCs Pack More Power:

the running of more complex software programs with larger output files. With successive generations of silicon microprocessor engines— Intel's 16-bit 286 and 386SX, 32-bit 386DX, 486 and 586—the desktop computer has taken on more of the characteristics of earlier mainframes, differing only in the number of input/output ports. The 586, called the *Pentium*, packs 3.1 million transistors in an area four times bigger than the 486. Each transistor is so tiny that it would take 500 of them to circle a human hair. The Pentium will crunch numbers like a mainframe, executing 100 million instructions per second—five times the speed of the 486.

The introduction of 100-MIPs computers on the desktop has already increased the load on the LAN. Next it will impact the WAN. Whereas 10 Mb/s Ethernet LANs are common, enterprise use of WAN bandwidth beyond T1 or 1.544 Mb/s is unusual. Bandwidth management has not kept up with new application demands and will continue to lag until there is more widespread use of broadband technology. For LANs, these demands have led to a new generation of LANs, operating at 100 Mb/s and above. For WANs, it has led to investment in the synchronous transmission technology provided by SONET/SDH, and faster switching fabrics provided by cell relay and ATM.

The interlocking relationship between more powerful computers and advanced software applications created the need for operating systems that make good use of the available computer power. A new generation of desktop operating systems—IBM's OS/2, Novell's UNIX, Microsoft's Windows NT, and Taligent's object-oriented OS, among others—support the increasingly widespread use of desktop imaging, voice annotation, and multimedia. Early microprocessors used 640 kilobytes of RAM in the personal computers that employed them. Now personal computers support four- to 16-megabytes of RAM. With these large amounts of memory and more powerful microprocessors, network users may now run on-line background applications that receive updated information in response to complex database queries. Computer companies have re-engineered their applications to support distributed client/server computing, which increases bandwidth demand even if application requirements remain constant. But the application bandwidths have also increased. Many applications employ multimedia, incorporating audio, images, and full-motion video as well as text. Today's cooperative software allows a single application to spawn many others. As they interact, they exact bandwidth from the network. Each computer MIP on the desk generates some demand for bandwidth. Even voice overlays consume valuable bandwidth: as a rule of thumb, four minutes of digitized voice takes four-megabytes of storage.

2.4.   MORE BROADBAND APPLICATIONS

If computing needs remained static, the narrowband WAN infrastructure and, consequently, the disparity between LANs and WANs, would probably continue for years to come. But this will change as bandwidth-hungry applications abound in everyday business activity. Consider the growing popularity of the intelligent building. By 1995, in Europe alone, investment in intelligent buildings is projected to reach $15 billion because it is possible to save up to 30% of building operating costs. This environment optimally integrates people, property, and technology by managing a variety of computer services on a local network. These islands of computer power then connect into the worldwide public telephone network. For the user, the way that information is accessed and the burden it places on the network remains transparent.

As applications such as the intelligent building proliferate, bandwidth demands upon the public network will increase. Regardless of the *size* of communication links, more connections will increasingly tax network capacity. Even LANs, with their relatively large megabit buses, are not immune to bandwidth overload. Ethernet, token ring and FDDI all share media—always a potential bottleneck. The shared LAN can bog down under the burden of large numbers of users and of information-intensive transfers. With so much information being shipped over a single route, the ability to manage and dynamically allocate it on the fly is critical. Individual users can be better served by having exclusive use of the bandwidth, rather than sharing it, and that is the basis for some of the new switching technologies and the driving force for new broadband transport technologies that can manage huge amounts of bandwidth.

2.4.1. Workgroup Software

Workgroup Software, sometimes referred to as *cooperative software* or *groupware*, allows a single action to generate a host of other actions automatically. It takes advantage of new, more powerful operating systems to make the physical topology of the network transparent to the user. Users no longer need a sense of where resources are on the network, or how they communicate. With this structure, all applications become workgroup applications, overcoming the constraints of time and distance.

Workgroup software boosts productivity by letting a firm leverage highly skilled people, relaying advice and analysis from specialists to the group. While increasing productivity, such software consumes large amounts of bandwidth between end-stations because bandwidth-intensive applications are spawned without user awareness (Figure 2.2). For example, Lotus Notes®, an E-mail system that runs under Windows, is based on an object-storage mechanism that uses replication technology to update remote copies of mail databases housed on a Notes server. It is also used for forms and images. Everyone on the network has an electronic bulletin board over which they can automatically send and receive information in whatever form they desire, to as many people as they want. Among other things, co-workers can share information (Figure 2.3). Marketing and sales groups can share a common database that tracks and monitors all contacts with a single customer. Accountants can share financial and tax information; secretaries can exchange letters; engineers can exchange design files. A single voucher on a computer can be simultaneously forwarded to a supervisor for approval and to a secretary for filing. When signed by the supervisor, it can automatically be sent to accounting where a voucher can be generated. In another instance, a team project can be coordinated by an electronic

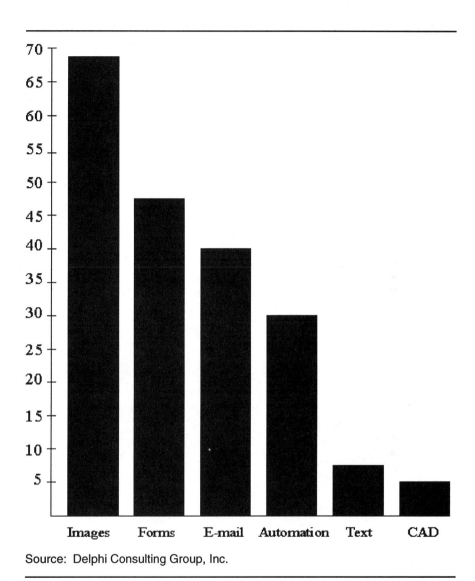

Source: Delphi Consulting Group, Inc.

Figure 2.2.   Cooperative software applications (in percentages).

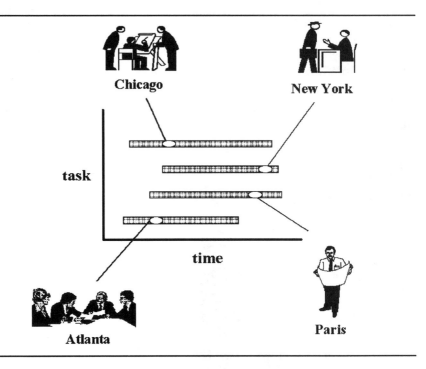

Figure 2.3. Workgroup interaction via the network.

schedule that automatically updates each member. The result is better and faster decision-making and an increase in the total volume of routine business transactions that traverse the network.

A workgroup program can improve a company's productivity, but some of its benefits also raise concerns (Table 2.3):

Table 2.3. Workgroup issues

Benefits	*Concerns*
gives end users broader access to data	lets workers know more than they should
flattens organizations, speeding decision making	threatens authority of chain of management
improves individuals' ability to collaborate	results in loss of individuals' recognition and competitive edge

It is interesting to note that similar concerns were raised by MIS managers when personal computers were introduced.

2.4.2. Multimedia and Hypertext

The goal of multimedia is to make networked computers handle sound, image, and video as readily as they handle numbers and text. Multimedia relies upon the electronic integration of different media to enhance the ability of users to interact with the information in a format that suits their immediate needs. However, multimedia is still expensive to implement because it requires the use of specialized peripherals such as CD-ROM or videodisk players, or VCRs. The standards are still being worked out, and many of today's microcomputers will not support the final standards (Table 2.4). Moreover, network managers wanting to implement applications that support high-quality, full-motion video require broadband networks. Even with compression, VHS-quality video takes 1.2 Mb/s of bandwidth and advanced digital video can use 30 to 130 Mb/s. LANs like Ethernet, accustomed to carrying data, have problems transporting full-motion video, which requires the delivery of packets in a particular order, with small, consistent delays. Packet video on LANs needs faster, isochronous protocols to deliver the continuous data streams of voice, video, and data with little delay. Such isochronous protocols establish a virtual channel that behaves like a dedicated point-to-point circuit between devices. Among the technologies competing for multimedia traffic are ATM, fast Ethernet and FDDI-II (detailed in chapters 4 and 6.)

Hypertext is a technological buzzword for a retrieval system in which individual words are indexed and threads created to have one word lead to another. In merging text and graphics and not requiring specialized computers, hypertext constitutes a logical migration point to multimedia. This level of integration would be highly useful in developing computerized training modules, for example. Hypertext is especially useful in conjunction with massive databases because it takes information retrieval to a new level by making it simpler to use and find. To accomplish this, many database vendors rely exclusively on Boolean searches to create indexes automatically that list the occurrence of every designated word or related sets of words in the database. While this capability is valuable, by itself it is not true hypertext. To create true hypertext, the contents of the database must be coded to link one subject with another.

Just as it took the installation of millions of LANs to create sufficient LAN traffic to impact the WAN, multimedia applications are now

Table 2.4.   Multimedia standards.

Standard	Proponent	What it does
Digital Video Interactive	Intel	Offers real-time video (RTV) and production level video (PLV) compression at a ratio of up to 160-to-1. RTV compresses video in real time, while PLV compresses stored video. RTV and PLV offer play back rates of 30 frames/second.
Quick Time	Apple Computer	Enables Macintosh users to create, store, transmit, and play back compressed video at rates between 15 and 30 frames/sec. Apple is transporting QuickTime to Microsoft Windows.
Video for Windows	Microsoft	Enables Windows users to create, store, transmit, and play back compressed video at rates between 15 and 30 frames/sec. Supports the Audio Visual Interleave compression standard.
MPEG	ISO's motion picture experts group	Several MPEG standards are being developed to format video clips at compression ratios from 50-to-1 up to 200-to-1.
JPEG	*CCITT and ISO's Joint Photographic Experts Group	JPEG has its roots in still–image compression and formatting and is now addressing full–motion video. The JPEG algorithm offers relatively high resolution and uses a compression ratio between 20-to-1 and 50-to-1.
Px64	CCITT	A suite of standards for video conferencing that includes the H.261 standard. Allows for connections between video conferencing codecs made by different vendors using single or multiple 64K bit/second circuits.

*CCITT, the Comite Consulatif Internationale Telegraphique et Telophonique, a United Nations International Telecommunications unit.

gathering critical mass. Hastening this process is the introduction of multimedia files that increase by four to 10 times in size each year due to the amount of charts, pictures and even voice that are being incorporated within the text. By 1997, 10% of the workstations sold in the United States will have multimedia capability, according to Information Strategies Group of Vienna, Va. Coupled with hypertext, use of that capability will increase network traffic. Every time such traffic enters the network, the demand for bandwidth increase—as does average network traffic load. Consequently, a major success factor for multimedia will be the availability of sufficient bandwidth to handle large numbers of multimedia applications. Although the full impact of multimedia applications is still several years away, the network infrastructure must be in place well in advance.

2.4.3. Videoconferencing

According to a recent American Express survey, U.S. businesses will spend over $120 billion on travel in 1992. Videoconferencing could substantially reduce business travel costs by transporting conversations and images instead of people. The savings can be significant. Video signals can be transmitted over private links, dedicated T1 and T3 links, and over the public telephone network. The difference is the degree to which the transmission can approximate full-motion video. One way to transmit video at lower bandwidths is with signal compression such as that specified by the Motion Pictures Expert Group (MPEG). Some compressed video uses image prediction algorithms that have trouble tracking rapid scene changes. Rather than the stop and start of slow-scan video, consumers favor transmissions that resemble what they see today on a television screen. For example, a broadband network-based videoconferencing system employing broadband switches can use multiple fixed cameras. Viewers can select which person they want on screen and the system will select the best angle and the right camera for the picture. The increased consumer acceptance of 'motion' video transported over broadband networks could jump-start the videoconferencing market, outweighing the increased cost for bandwidth.

2.4.4. Image Processing

Researchers estimate that 95% of the world's information resides on paper or microfilm. The task of moving data from these dated technologies to electronic form is done by image processing systems. Image processing converts existing documents of all kinds to digital representations, which can be viewed quickly on a computer monitor, printed, or distributed in a variety of ways. This includes maps, fingerprints, CAT scans, drawings, and anything else that can be represented in two dimensions. The components of a basic image processing system include scanners resembling fax machines that make a digital record of every small sector (called dots) of an existing document, a controlling computer (microcomputer, minicomputer or mainframe), a monitor, and storage. In most networks, the efficient use of storage media such as optical disks and jukeboxes is pivotal to a successful imaging system. The high gigabyte content of most platters is essential to archiving libraries of documents because a single, high-resolution image can consume tens of megabytes of storage. In addition, document imaging systems can mix data, photographs, and full-motion video.

Imaging is often viewed simply as a storage and retrieval vehicle, but imaging systems can completely transform the way an organization operates. Consider the impact of image transfer on productivity. Federal agencies that handle huge numbers of documents are embracing electronic imaging. In fact, image processing has been used widely in the federal government since the mid-1980s, replacing microfilm and microfiche, which employ photographic technology. The handling of financial records and contracts is the top application for the federal government. Here, the technology reduced the storage space needed for documents by a factor of 12 *and* allowed quicker retrieval. For the IRS alone, there is the potential to save $41 million a year in the storage and retrieval of paper documents.

Given today's technology, it remains a big challenge to shuttle hundreds of megabytes of images across the enterprise network. The digital storage requirements of a single full-color image can exceed 16 megabytes, providing the detail for the rich variations of color and texture in fine artwork. Experts in the U.S. could study great works of art in Russia without leaving their terminals. The transfer of such large files over a public or private network requires bandwidths that provide a tolerable amount of delay or transmission time—that is, the hours or seconds required to complete the file transfer.

The transfer time depends on the amount of network bandwidth used. Higher bandwidths cost more. In the case of specialists such as art assessors or medical radiologists, their time alone may be worth the increased network costs. For other businesses, the increased cost of bandwidth is justified by considerable overall savings in other operations. Take worldwide catalog sales, for instance. Instead of producing costly monthly paper catalog updates in several languages, central image storehouses can be accessed by users in different countries across high-speed, real-time links. One of the world's largest pizza restaurant chains has managed to cut response time to suppliers from five days to 10 minutes, while receiving a 16% after-tax return on investment. A network of imaging equipment tracks fixed assets and handles the more than 10,000 faxed invoices it receives from worldwide suppliers each month. As invoices come into their accounts payable department, they are scanned into the imaging system. Over 40 workstations, connected by fiber optic cabling to servers interconnected by means of an Ethernet LAN, access two mainframes. On the mainframe computers reside databases that store the locations of restaurants and can identify more than 90,000 vendors.

2.4.5. Optical Computers

Introduced in the 1950's, silicon integrated circuits have transported much of the world from the Industrial Revolution to the Information Age. Many believe that the next great leap will come from the marriage of light and electricity in the optical computer, which is already under investigation. A prototype developed at the University of Colorado consists of lasers, electronic switches and optical fibers arranged in layers and stuffed into an area about the size of a desk. As in electronic computers, information is represented by binary ones and zeros. The optical computer uses the presence or absence of light pulses to represent the binary pattern. The prototype optical computer operates at a clock rate of 50 Mb/s, controlling a 16-bit microprocessor. Data-encoded light pulses are stored in some three miles of spooled fiber cable. Each bit of information is carried in a 12-foot long light pulse, which traverses the memory spool every 20 millionths of a second. The pulses are synchronized by the unvarying speed of light. From such prototypes a number of information age applications may emerge, including:

* A high-speed graphics processor that uses millions of optical switches interconnected in free space with mirrors rather than fiber cable. This type of computer can interconnect a virtually unlimited number of optical switches—at least in theory.
* A 20 Gb/s optical computer on a single silicon wafer.

2.4.6. Mobile Computing

The marriage of the communications, computer, and consumer electronics industries is rapidly creating products that allow people to transfer data without wires. Wireless communications are made possible by the emerging electronic superhighway along with the services, products, and information that will use it. The growth in wireless data is driven by the proliferation of portable computers, LANs, client/server computing, spread spectrum and cellular telephony, and the falling cost of data transmission with broadband networks. This blend of personal communications technologies is creating the mobile professional—an employee untethered by place or time. In 1992, only half a million of over 36 million mobile devices were data-oriented. This is changing (Table 2.5).

Wireless data communication is freeing workers from traditional constraints. Mobile applications such as the officeless desktop, one- and two-way messaging, long-distance file uploads, and the ubiquitous E-mail allow them to reach anyone, anywhere. Consider the benefits of wireless E-mail: it can always find individuals; business deals can be negotiated while in transit; people stay in touch with the home office and with clients. Messages can be initiated and responded to when and where people want. Wireless E-mail may be the most significant tool for the mobile professional, replacing pagers and cellular telephones—as well as airport and hotel room searches for RJ-11 jacks!

2.4.7. Home Video

Although local cable companies offer limited versions of home video, only the more comprehensive switched network can offer universal

Table 2.5. Wireless Communications: Projected Number of U.S. Users.

	1993	*1994*	*1995*	*1996*
Cellular (voice and data)	13 M	16 M	19 M	22 M
Personal communications systems (voice)	100,000	500,000	1 M	1.5 M
Paging	15.2 M	17.2 M	19.2 M	22 M
Wireless packet data services	1.3 M	1.7 M	2.5 M	3.3 M
Mobile computers	23,000	75,000	255,000	795,000
Personal digital assistants (voice and data)	2,000	22,000	94,000	289,000

Source: The Yankee Group

video access. Despite the desirability of this service, fiber optic connections to the home are not being made as fast as many experts originally predicted because of the traditional time for planning and study incurred by local exchange carriers (LECs). The stakes are large. There are potentially 140 million access lines in the US alone, which could cost $1,000 each to convert.

However, this market is now expected to expand rapidly. Government regulators have allowed the LECs to enter the home video market and, in return, the local loop has been opened to competition from alternate access providers and cable companies. A steady stream of projects is getting under way with the goal of merging PC and TV technologies, creating a super information appliance. Fiber optic vendors, cable TV operators and telephone companies are teaming up. All want to be among the first to install fiber optic cable to carry a variety of services to the home market. One of the first, Cablevision of Woodbury, New York, will hook up 100,000 of its subscribers on Long Island in 1994 and its remaining one million subscribers by the end of 1995.

Digital TV broadcasts will enable intelligent video dial tone systems. Such systems go beyond today's pay-per-view, which requires a user to call up the cable company to sign up for a movie that the cable company has scheduled for broadcast. With video dial tone, a viewer uses a remote control to program the TV to capture and download a movie from a menu of movies. When the movie ends, the viewer can download other information—from a shopping network, for example.

The race is on to build an electronic superhighway capable of delivering hundreds of new TV channels, as well as data and phone services. Once the loop is opened, and low-capacity systems are upgraded to support broadband transmission, the path will be cleared for electronic encyclopedias, shopping catalogs, travel, banking services and more, all brought to the home on a real-time basis. Full-range audio and high-resolution video-on-demand will make home entertainment an entirely new experience. At the same time, video to the home will also open the way to truly effective telecommuting, favorably impacting the performances of the more than 30 million home-based businesses in the United States.

2.4.8. Voice Processing

Voice processing encompasses a number of separate but related technologies, including voice messaging, voice response, interactive/transactional voice response, text-to-speech, voice recognition, and synthesis. Most voice automation systems use digital technology to store, retrieve and manipulate voice signals. The market for all voice processing equipment nearly tripled from 1987 to 1990, from $800 million to more than $2.2 billion. Voice mail has traditionally been the leading application of voice processing technology, and the market for voice mail systems is expected to reach $1.5 billion by 1993, according to the Stamford, Conn. market research Gartner Group. Voice mail is becoming just one more component in a broader voice processing system. Voice mail as a solitary application is yielding to multiple applications. Many systems have auto attendant, voice mail, audiotext, IVR and other applications available simultaneously.

Of all the applications for voice processing technology, interactive voice response (IVR) systems are the fastest growing market segment and the second largest market sector, after voice mail. The IVR market is growing at an annual rate of 25%, whereas the voice mail annual growth rate has leveled off to 16%. If this trend continues, IVR equipment sales will lead the market by 1995.

The IVR caller typically keys information on a touch-tone telephone. With transactional systems, a more sophisticated form of IVR, users can input information to a host database. For example, a caller who uses voice response to check on his or her customer file and locates an error in the database can leave a voice message detailing the discrepancy without having to call the company again. Integrated systems also offer advantages for internal users: traveling sales representatives calling their own phones back at the office can receive an order previously left on their voice mail and check the company's database to determine the availability of the desired item in a *single* telephone call. Perhaps the most exciting application is to combine IVR with the personal computer for forms processing (Figure 2.4).

There is a growing integration of telecommunications and PCs. A voice processing system is essentially a specially equipped computer system, but telephone companies have not integrated voice mail effectively with computers because telephones are treated like commodities in most businesses. Future desktop systems will combine the telephone and microcomputer into a tightly integrated desktop unit. Moreover, the advent of portable personal communicators will provide hand-held voice mail capability. Users could make telephone calls through the PC by clicking on an icon to place, receive, put calls on hold, or play calls back.

2.4.8.1. Hardware & Software.   PC-based systems are equipped with a processor, multiple port I/O cards, hard disk drives, monitor, keyboard, and voice processing software. The system connects to Centrex, key sys-

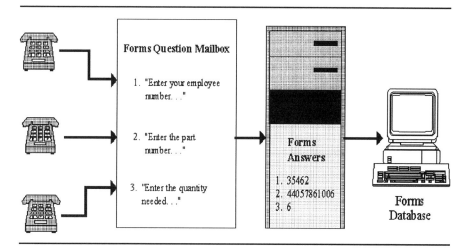

Figure 2.4.   Automated forms processing.

tems, or PBXs through a single line extension or PBX interface. PC-based systems provide:

1. a database for voice storage,
2. network interfaces (modem, CSU/DSU) that allow the caller's telephone to function as an input/output node on a network, and
3. menu-driven application generators that enable users to customize their voice processing applications.

The fundamental hardware component is the voice card. The voice card plugs into an empty expansion slot in an *off-the-shelf* PC (Figure 2.5). The card converts voice and other analog signals into a digital format and connects to the telephone network. The card also connects to the internal computer bus as well as its own voice bus.[1] This bus is used by other plug-in cards that provide fax, voice recognition, and text-to-speech conversion. New add-on products bring the human voice to personal computing to enhance E-mail, word processing, and spread-

---

[1] A voice bus is independent of the computer controlling the card and allows audio as well as signaling information to be passed between different voice processing components.

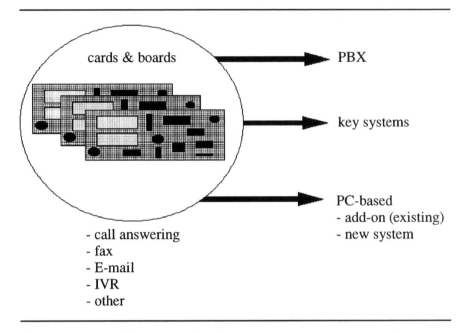

Figure 2.5.   Voice card applications.

sheet analysis. The products capture short voice recordings and attach them to a message or document for later replay to emphasize or expand on text and images. The PC and the voice card by themselves do not form a voice processing system. Additional hardware and software is required for other applications (Table 2.6). Voice messaging software runs under popular PC operating systems such as MS-DOS and UNIX.

2.4.8.2 Applications.   Subscribers simply dial into the messaging service to pick up or drop off information. Received messages can be automatically distributed according to customer schedules. Although voice mail has been combined with other forms of messaging—E-mail and EDI, among others—voice and fax integration in particular have been picking up steam. While applications development is still in its infancy, two general areas have emerged:

- Integrated messaging, which merges fax, voice, and E-mail in one subscriber's mailbox. Upon interrogating the mailbox, the subscriber is informed that a mix of messages is waiting.

Table 2.6. Voice processing system.

Hardware	
computer	ground start interface
loop start interface	T1 interface
direct inward dialing	speech recognition card
fax card	station adapters
audio multiplexers	audio couplers
audio interfaces	

Software	
operating system	speech analyzers
development	device drivers
speech library	compilers
debugger	call progress programs
diagnostic software	voice prompt editors

• Information dissemination, which, in most small systems, consists of audiotext; IVR is beginning to evolve.

2.4.8.3. Integration. PC-based products can be interfaced to a key system, PBX system, another PC, or to a LAN or WAN. Although today's LANs do not carry voice traffic, they can be used to combine PCs to increase processing power. And in the near term, LAN bandwidths will increase tenfold, allowing voice as well as data traffic to be transported. Scientific advances in photonics and silicon have contributed to a new age that is characterized by desktop to LAN-to-WAN communications. WANs become extended LANs. ATM switches that allow concurrent routing of voice with data are already available.[2] These work equally well in LANs and WANs.

---

[2]To most of us, an ATM is where we do our banking. But this technology is entering the market and promising to undo the hitherto inviolate separation of data and voice.

2.5.   Supporting Technology

Scientific advances in photonics and silicon have contributed to a new age that will be characterized by desktop supercomputers linked by networks that communicate at tens and even hundreds of gigabits per second (Gb/s). The virtual freedom from error and the high speed of fiber optics, coupled with powerful and economical desktop computers, have triggered a paradigm shift in which the WAN has become a homogenous extension of the LAN: enter the era of ultra-high speed, stripped down communication protocols and concurrent networking.

2.5.1.   Fiber Optic Cable

The bandwidth capacity of fiber is now being exploited for digital transmission. Thinner than a human hair yet stronger than steel, fiber has become the basic media for long-haul and interoffice telecommunications networks. The special characteristic of optical fiber is its low impedance to lightwaves and its tremendous modulation capacity, supporting higher bandwidths over longer distances—enough to accommodate tens of thousands of voice channels. Researchers have transported information at rates exceeding 350 Gb/s. At that rate, the entire content of 1.2 million books could be transported around the globe in a minute! Unquestionably, one of the most dramatic changes in telecommunications over the last decade is the vast amount of fiber embedded in the public network, which provides almost unlimited bandwidth potential.

The fastest commercial fiber-based system today launches pulses down a fiber cable at roughly 2.5 billion pulses per second at much lower error rates (10^{-12}) than the error rates (10^{-8}) for the copper it replaces. This permits high speed protocols that would not have worked over the error-prone copper lines. It also makes the simultaneous transmission of high-resolution video, digital audio, and data possible in two distinct network environments:

- In the WAN environment, fiber supports two types of high-capacity networks; asynchronous T3 at 45 Mb/s (European E3 is 34 Mb/s), and synchronous optical networks (SONET in North America, SDH in Europe) with defined rates of 2.5 Gb/s, but capable of tens of gigabits per second.
- For LAN connectivity, it is being used as the means of extending traditional shared media LANs via the fiber distributed data interface (FDDI) and metropolitan area networks (MANs) based on IEEE and Bellcore standards.

This has created a demand for two types of fiber optic cable, single-mode and multi-mode. Single-mode fiber cable is used in the public WAN for several reasons. Information travels greater distances on it without requiring repeaters, and it removes the bandwidth limitations of multi-mode fiber (which runs out of steam above 155 Mb/s). On the other hand, multi-mode fiber cable is likely to be found in buildings because it simplifies installation, lowers cost, and is supported by major computer companies. Consequently, multi-mode fiber cable has become the favorite for fiber LANs such as FDDI.

2.5.2. Shared Versus Concurrent Media Technologies

Today's heterogeneous LAN and WAN networks evolved from a mix of networking technologies that were developed for different reasons. The public telephone network served primarily as a voice transport, while the LAN evolved in the early 1970s to support data traffic. For this reason, LAN and WAN traffic and the technologies that support them have differed substantially. Technologies designed to accommodate bursty LAN traffic are inappropriate for carrying real-time voice and video traffic that not only consume bandwidth, but have a low tolerance for delay. The situation is changing as broadband applications develop; they are forcing all network topologies—local, metropolitan and wide area—to accommodate them. In the not-so-distant future, LAN traffic may be significantly different. Instead of predominantly packet-based data traffic, LANs may carry significant amounts of real-time traffic generated by multimedia voice and video applications.

Shared-media technologies such as packet switching, Ethernet, token ring, and FDDI provide momentary access to a communications route and are appropriate for bursts of heavy communications traffic and periods of low activity. The route is used only as needed, allowing its cost to be spread among many users. Since this topology is susceptible to failure if a single station hogs the line, these networks use arbitration schemes for determining when stations can transmit.

Shared media can carry video traffic if there is no multi-access arbitration between the workstation and the hub. In other words, video traffic can be supported if there is only one user on each segment. But this situation does not often occur in a shared environment. Consequently, shared-media LANs are not employed for latency-sensitive voice and video transfers. More appropriate transports include WAN isochronous networks that are synchronized to a real-time clock. Isochronous transport is a way to transmit such asynchronous information by synchronous means. Voice traffic is often transported by isochronous networks because conversations do not occur in regular, predictable intervals. One form of isochronous transport is the concurrent network.

Circuit switching and other concurrent technologies use dedicated routes to exploit the full-route bandwidth. The cost of the service is high because the user pays for the bandwidth even when it is not being used. Emerging switched services are not the answer for the user who needs continuous access for a major portion of the day, since they are priced higher than dedicated route service. Therefore, switched services are used primarily for route back-up. On the other hand, new broadband technologies combine the best features of shared and dedicated transmission media, making them useful for both LANs and WANs. ATM, for example, uses fixed-length cell-relay transmissions and buffering to ensure that multimedia applications are guaranteed a fixed response time, which is required to support real-time voice and video transmissions. With ATM, the media is not shared, it is switched, allowing each user full bandwidth as they use the circuit. ATM also employs dynamically variable circuits through which sequential data packets can be routed on a point-to-point basis, rather than broadcasting traffic to every node on the network, as in shared media, or having a single application use the entire bandwidth, as in circuit switching. Users can almost 'dial up' whatever capacity they need in real-time for the type of service desired.

2.5.3. Silicon Integration

The LAN revolution became reality when Xerox's Ethernet became a *de facto* standard with the backing of DEC and Intel. DEC supplied the customer base and Intel supplied the integrated circuits that resulted in affordable connection devices. The result was a form of broadband network—the LAN.[A] High technology markets are fueled by the economies afforded by integrated circuits. Silicon architectures that duplicate simple atomic elements to form massively parallel systems are the basis for modern broadband technologies. With simple solutions in silicon, larger and more complex systems are economically possible. One result is the rapid evolution of the microprocessor, which is the engine of modern computers. These silicon chips continue to increase in function, power, and speed. The microprocessor has grown from the four-bit

---

[A]For some, the term *broadband network* evokes memories of the early LAN implementations that used multiple frequencies to transmit data over coaxial cable. Even today one of the largest applications of broadband networking is in the cable TV industry where multiple channels are broadcast to millions of households.

bus of the 1970s to the eight- and 16-bit bus of the 1980s, to the 32-bit bus of the 1990s. Today microprocessors using 64-bit buses are on the near horizon, creating integrated circuits that possess the processing power limited to the mainframe computer only a few years ago.

Computer power is not the only factor; the price of computer components has dropped considerably. If these trends continue, it will be possible to embed massive intelligence into everyday appliances. A future interactive television costing only a few hundred dollars could incorporate a 32 bit microprocessor and 16 megabytes of memory. With a connection to a broadband network based upon SONET/SDH and ATM chip sets, the television could present a friendly graphical interface with full motion video and voice response. It could transparently search for programs. A student in New York City could learn Japanese with text from a data bank in Tokyo overlayed with images from an image bank in London—all in real-time.

2.5.4. Wireless Communications

A variety of new technologies are beginning to enable remote users to connect to LANs without telephone lines, and to enable LANs themselves to operate without cabling. Wireless LANs that connect PC nodes in different buildings work in fundamentally the same way that wired networks do. Communications systems must perform two basic actions: encode information in a form that is understandable by both sender and receiver, and carry the encoded information from source to destination. Computer communications systems encrypt data according to an agreed upon protocol that usually includes some method of error correction. Moving the encoded information without wires relies on transfer techniques using electromagnetic radiation, radio waves, or infrared light.

Although wireless networks employ infrared and radio transmission, radio waves are most often used to interconnect LANs. Network signals are carried on electromagnetic waves for both wired and radio wave LANs, but radio networks usually use frequencies between 902 MHz and 928 MHz, which is about nine times the maximum frequency that coaxial cable can carry. Radio networks require more elaborate error-prevention techniques than other networks because signals in the air cannot be shielded from interference. To internetwork wired LANs by means of radio waves, a special network driver and interface card reside in a gateway. The card uses a digital-to-analog converter to translate the LAN's binary signals into analog waves. These analog waves are sent to a radio transceiver (transmitter/receiver), where they then modulate radio carrier waves that are transmitted to the other LAN.

Spread-spectrum radio, a common wireless technique, overcomes interference problems by sending broadcasts over a spread of frequencies instead of using a single focused frequency. The Federal Communications Commission, which regulates frequency assignments for spread-spectrum, is allowing frequencies previously reserved for industrial, scientific, and military use to be used for data networks.

Using spread-spectrum, the signal is sent across a broad bandwidth of frequencies to minimize the danger of data loss and thus the need to retransmit the data, which would slow the network. In one type of spread-spectrum transmission, *signal hopping*, sophisticated transceivers send data for a few milliseconds on one frequency, then change to another. In a further attempt to reduce data loss, this type of spread-spectrum transmission uses redundancy and sends the same data on several different frequencies in case interference corrupts the signal.

The receiving gateway on the second LAN employs a second transceiver to remove the signal from the carrier wave. An analog-to-digital converter in the network card converts the signal to binary code. In the LAN gateway, the data is pieced together and undergoes statistical checks called 'checksums' to ensure that it has arrived uncorrupted. If the checksum when the signal is received does not agree with the one generated when the signal was sent, the receiving gateway requests that the data be sent again.

2.6.   CONCLUSION

There is no single reason why the demand for broadband services has accelerated. Certainly the global competitive environment, where businesses must be well informed and nimble to survive, has fueled it. The growth of personal computers and sophisticated software applications that make businesses more efficient and effective is another contributor, because these pockets of information must be interconnected. Workgroup software allows users to share knowledge in the form of images, video, and text. Workgroups and entire companies automatically spawn network messages that track customers, create conferences, and access a library of policies, documentation, and news. Never before has the networking of computers or the ability to message anywhere and anytime been so important to business success. And never before has the torrent of bandwidth demands deluged public and private networks, pressing for intelligent and concurrently managed information superhighways. This has created an explosive market for new broadband networks, equipment, and carrier services.

3

Elements of Broadband Networks

3.1. INTRODUCTION

Broadband markets rely on the tremendous growth of desktop computers and fiber cable to bolster the demand for emerging equipment and services. In the past decade, the bandwidth of many business networks increased beyond one Mb/s. LANs went from one Mb/s ArcNet to 16 Mb/s token ring and are moving to even higher-speed 100 Mb/s FDDI. WANs increased from 64 kb/s to 1.544 Mb/s (T1) to 44.736 Mb/s (T3). Even higher-rate SONET/SDH connections are becoming available. The dramatic demand for high bandwidth stems from the equally impressive increase in demand for personal computers, whose worldwide numbers exceed 125 million. Both are fueled by steep decreases in computer hardware costs because of integrated circuit economies, and more sophisticated software applications. Soon, 100 MIPS desktop computers will be common, graphics resolution will increase twenty-fold, video quality six-fold, and large file transfers such as CAD/CAM a hundred-fold. In addition, message size will increase five-fold, while actual network transit time will decrease by over 30%. The cumulative result will be unprecedented growth in broadband markets.

One spin-off will be a market for broadband LAN equipment such as a low-cost switching system that operates at rates exceeding 155 Mb/s. Another will be for broadband services that will use a new Telco/PTT transmission and switching fabric (Table 3.1). But customers will need to understand their options for LANs and WANs, and providers will

Table 3.1.   Data applications and Telco/PTT services.

Application	Traffic	Service
data internetworking	large amount of aggregate traffic, steady average flow	continuous bit rate— SONET, T1
LAN internets	distributed traffic bursts at high rates	SMDS, frame relay, ATM
multimedia, voice and video	delay intolerant, high rates over short duration	ATM real–time services such as BISDN

need to understand the market dynamics. The customers who prosper in the 1990s will be the ones who solicit the combinations of features and services uniquely appropriate to their businesses. The providers who prosper will be the ones who offer these combinations.

3.2.   CHANGING BUSINESS NETWORKS

Large corporations use several networks, each with a distinct purpose: one for voice, another for SNA traffic, and possibly another for LAN traffic. Telco/PTT network architects face the daunting task of consolidating these diverse networks onto a single broadband fabric. Their reward will be an increase in data traffic beyond today's growth rate of 20% a year. It is not so much this increase as the changing nature of the traffic that is significant. Businesses are flourishing and withering on the basis of changes in data transactions. Witness the growth of facsimile service. Today, we are sending our letters over the Telco/PTT to the detriment of the postal service. The process continues to gain momentum as an increasing number of workers undertake data-intensive operations from their homes.

3.2.1.   Telecommuting, E-mail, and Facsimile

Telecommuting has long been touted as the solution to traffic jams, the energy crisis, and as a way to increase productivity. In 1988, Arthur D. Little, the management consulting firm, estimated that teleworking could save the U.S. economy $23 billion per year. The inevitability of telecommuting is being aided by the political process. Today, 108 million Americans commute to work by car, an increase of more than 30% since 1980. The Clean Air Act of 1990 tried to reduce car commuting by 25% in the most polluted U.S. cities. As highway traffic lessens, telecommuting will contribute to data build-up in the public network—a situation that the growing acceptance of messaging technologies such as E-mail and fax will exacerbate.

The economies and efficiencies of electronic messaging are becoming more widely appreciated, making geographically dispersed businesses easier to operate and manage. Today, progressive companies use electronic messaging to keep in touch with employees, customers, and vendors, overcoming the barriers of time and distance and enhancing business relationships. In the petrochemical and transportation industries, many companies have already found that using messaging to augment and complement voice conversations not only improves partner relationships but reduces the time and cost of making decisions. They rely on electronic messaging because of the inherent interdependency of their businesses. One company alone has 28,000 corporate users that communicate with 12 million electronic mailboxes worldwide. For this company, there was never any question about extending their successful corporate messaging system to the outside; the problem was how to implement it to serve their customers and suppliers better. Proprietary solutions were quickly discarded as it became apparent that only an international, public messaging network could keep pace with technology advances, work with the company's existing hardware, and allow users of equipment from various vendors to communicate. The solution was to connect their internal system to a public messaging network that consolidated and managed their faxes and E-mail, thus ensuring that both internal and external communications were simpler, more effective, and future-proof.

3.2.2. Social Impact

The delivery of information in all its forms—text, image, and video—promises an unprecedented level of educational, health, and entertainment services on a worldwide scale. The explosive growth in the number of home-based businesses, estimated to be 30 million in the United States alone, is a direct result of their being able to compete via the global telecommunications network. Home-based businesses are not the only ones making innovative use of the telecommunications network. Traditional businesses have discovered that the savings in time and labor are well worth the investment in electronic messaging. They are finding that freedom from geographic and time constraints is crucial for competing in global markets. This view also extends to nations.

The European community intends to strengthen the interoperability of existing networks and reinforce its economic and social aims at the same time. The Maastricht Treaty, signed in 1991 by members of the Commission of European Communities (CEC), proclaimed that the community shall "contribute to the establishment of trans-European networks in the areas of transport, telecommunications and energy infrastructures." This infrastructure will provide a common point of dissemination for knowledge, culture, and history of the European people. Broadband networks are faster and more intelligent than the LANs and WANs they replace. Comparatively speaking, their improvements over earlier networks are as sweeping as those of the fax over the earlier telex. The ability to manage information and provide bandwidth on demand liberates users from time constraints, improves relationships within organizations, and decreases the costs of gathering and dispersing information.

Less developed countries, too, have the opportunity to leapfrog into broadband communications—terrestrial fiber, synchronous transport, scaleable protocols—gaining benefits perhaps *before* more developed countries that have a considerable investment in their existing asynchronous network infrastructures. Developing countries, for example, could end up with telecommunications networks that are superior to those in Europe or North America, providing them with a framework for economic competition.

3.3.   HIGH-SPEED MAINFRAME INTERFACES

Although the hierarchical computer networks of the 1980s have grudgingly given way to LANs, the need for direct high speed linkage to a mainframe port remains. High-speed serial channel interface (HSSI) has gradually been accepted as an important physical interface and a *de facto* industry standard for serial transmission at rates reaching 52 Mb/s between data terminal and communications equipment. HSSI defines the physical layer for transmission but does not define the transmission protocol, allowing computability with emerging high-speed network services such as SMDS. Instead of using the interface to link routers to point-to-point T3 lines, HSSI provides a way to connect routers to meshed SMDS networks. In contrast, alternative ways for high speed-channel connection—Fibre Channel and Escon—define architectures for sending data over dedicated connections at distances of 500 meters to 10 kilometers and at speeds from 17 to 133 Mb/s, respectively.

3.4.   CPE: CONNECTING TO THE NETWORK

Modern communications networks satisfy the desktop-to-desktop service demands of users. A network is formed from Customer Premises Equipment (CPE) at customer locations, transmission equipment that is part of the network, switching equipment that forms the network routing fabric, and management elements that provide provisioning and control. There are a variety of environments (Figure 3.1) for CPE. Although there are instances of a single personal computer or terminal connecting to the network, for broadband networks it is more likely that traffic will be generated from a LAN.

3.4.1.   The Local Environment

Over the past two decades, proprietary computer architectures and protocols have kept customers captive. Unable to select the best equipment for the task, they were forced to purchase from a single vendor. The rise of LANs has broken these chains because LANs allow computer equip-

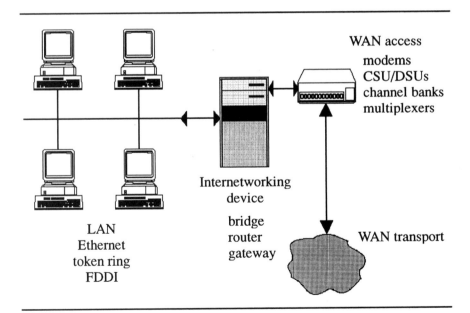

Figure 3.1.   CPE networking components.

ment from different vendors to be interconnected. Connections to the LAN are achieved with interfaces or adapters that plug into each device on the network—usually PCs, workstations, printers, or servers—and allow them to communicate with other devices. Some LANs exist as completely separate networks. What is more likely is that LAN traffic is pooled at an interface such as a bridge, router, or gateway to access devices on *other* LANs. These serve as the interface with the WAN, if the device being accessed is remotely located. Since the transmission protocols employed by LANs are effective over relatively small distances, the interface must convert between the LAN and WAN transmission protocols. Also, protocols employed by the computers being accessed may differ from those employed by transmitting devices. In the past, the numbers of different communications protocols have hindered conversation between devices. One of the promises of broadband communications is the lessening of the differences between communication protocols as the protocols employed by LANs and WANs coalesce. Likewise, the promotion of open architectures and protocols in the broadband WAN promises ubiquitous equipment and services.

3.4.2. Transport Environment

Information transported over the public telephone network may be in analog or digital form. Analog transport is used for low-speed voice, while digital signals that are represented by binary ones and zeros are used for data as well as voice transport. There is no inherent superiority of one format over another. Moreover, real-world information is usually in analog form. Nonetheless, for high-speed transmission purposes, the digital format is preferred because it is the natural environment for computing. Once information is converted to digital form, it can be manipulated and transported by digital machinery that takes advantage of the economies and efficiencies of silicon integrated circuits. Access from a private network, such as a LAN, into a public network is done by means of dial-up and private lines. Most telephones dial-up the public switched telephone network (PSTN), while data terminals that require continuous connection may use transmission lines that are leased from the telephone company. Sometimes a pair of terminal devices are connected by means of a private line that is dedicated to them. For example, a bank teller terminal in a remote branch may be connected to the mainframe computer at a central location this way. What is more likely is that the terminals will be connected by means of the public switched network.

3.4.3. Switching Environment

Switching systems employed in the LAN or WAN provides economical connectivity. Ideally, any terminal device connected to the network can communicate with any other. Large-scale interconnection often requires a hierarchy of switches. For example, the North American system employed by the PSTN uses a series of offices where the switches are housed (Figure 3.2). The class 5 office serves the local loop, which is the most common means for subscribers to interconnect with the public network. Here information from low-rate telephone lines is combined with high-usage trunks. These trunks form the broadband portion of the existing asynchronous public network and may achieve rates of one gigabit per second. Although synchronous transmission using SONET/

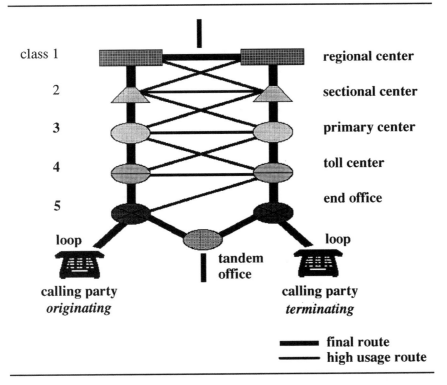

Figure 3.2.   Switching hierarchy.

SDH has higher bandwidths, the issue is not just the transport rates, but the *management* of such large bandwidths.

3.4.4. Management

Broadband equipment can handle an incredible amount of information. For the most part, effective management of such large amounts of information requires a tiered network architecture, beginning with equipment with enough intelligence to be managed, and reaching to the host and public carrier management systems. Initially, network management was concerned with homogeneous element-to-element communication. As networks grew in complexity, concerns about element configuration, performance statistics, and alarms led to a class of manager that provided central control of remote network elements. Security, disaster recovery, and reliability are all modern network management considerations, particularly with regard to broadband networks. Synchronous SONET/SDH devices have the intelligence to gather information about their own failure conditions, measure the performance of signals that pass through them, and assign bandwidth. They can determine their own failure as well as the failure of other network elements. The operations support system (OSS) that controls these elements must be able to interpret this information and take appropriate action. The Telco/PTT OSS, which in the past has not been concerned with the customer premises, is now beginning to interact with the management systems employed by private networks. The result will be desktop-to-desktop management of data.

3.5.   CONCLUSION

The data communications equipment industry is experiencing exciting new applications such as facsimile, E-mail, imaging, groupware, and multimedia. During this period, societal as well as economic pressures will continue to drive the computer and telecommunications industries in the same direction. Trends expanding the home workforce such as telecommuting, and legislative initiatives promoting the use of the telecommunications networks, are already creating unrivaled opportunities for broadband technologies and services. This will create a global demand for broadband networks that will change the business productivity equation. These networks will radically alter the boundaries between LANs and WANs as they provide a new format for information transport, switching, and management.

4

LANs

4.1. INTRODUCTION

LANs have emerged as the dominant computing environment, replacing earlier mainframe and minicomputer networks. The LAN was initially an assembly of wires and smaller computers that together created a more powerful computing environment. The ability of LANs to connect disparate equipment has elevated them to more than mere alternative cabling schemes. The successful IEEE LAN standardization made Ethernet and token ring into the most common LAN types. Both combine a variety of personal computers, workstations, servers, and peripheral devices into a seamless network. The LAN may attach ordinary telephone station wire to each device on the network, connecting in a wire closet to a backbone co-axial cable between floors, and possibly a fiber link between buildings (Figure 4.1). A new and powerful network element is the server. The server provides the interface between a user and a service such as printing or database storage. A variety of computer devices ranging from beefed-up PCs to data switches may be used as LAN servers, provided they are equipped with the appropriate interfaces. The sharing of information and equipment gives LANs great economy, allowing the LAN to emerge from the backwaters to the forefront of networking.

The emphasis has shifted from a single customer premises to interoperability of multivendor systems encompassing LANs and WANs. Unlike the WAN, the LAN spans a limited distance, often within a

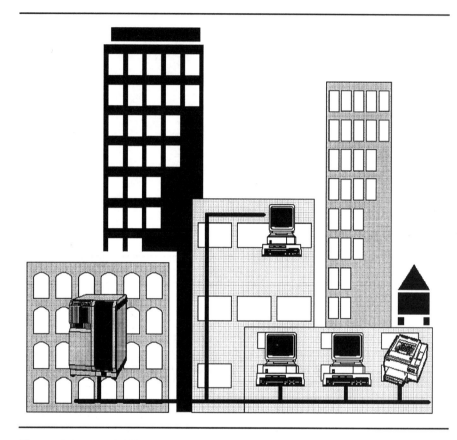

Figure 4.1.   LANs provide a powerful and efficient solution for campus and local area networking.

single building or group of buildings. But it is becoming less likely for users to be concerned only with their immediate environment. Today, they want to communicate and share resources and information independent of geographic constraints. This encourages the development of better interfaces between LANs and WANs as well as higher data rates.

4.2.   LAN OPERATION

The LAN is actually an early form of broadband network. It resembles a broadband WAN in terms of raw speed and distance. LANs transport information at rates up to 100 Mb/s. Moreover, they employ data error protection and congestion control mechanisms similar to those proposed for new broadband WANs. Both frame and cell relay are new WAN technologies that have borrowed from the LAN. The LAN does not send information in store-and-forward fashion with error detection and re-transmissions. The LAN transports data by means of simple address-ing and frame manipulation. The information to be transported is encapsulated within a frame that contains the addresses needed for network routing and management. The LAN protocols arbitrate the shared medium to permit devices on the network to communicate.

To the network architect, the LAN represents an island of intercon-nected computers. There are two general categories of LAN-related equip-ment: intra- and inter-LAN. The intra-LAN gear consists primarily of servers and network interface units that provide services and link termi-nals to the LAN bus. Inter-LAN products—bridges, routers and gate-ways—connect different LANs. LANs differ in terms of topology access method, connection hardware, media, operating systems, and protocols. Topology has the greatest impact upon installation, expansion, and oper-ating costs.

4.2.1. Topology

Network topology refers to physical and logical layout. The common LAN topologies are bus, ring, and star (Figure 4.2). Each topology influences the performance of a LAN as well as its use in enterprise networks.

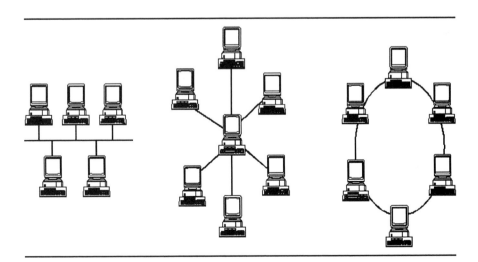

Figure 4.2.   Bus, star, and ring LAN topologies.

Table 4.1.   Common LAN topologies

Topology	IEEE standard	
bus	802.3	Ethernet
star	802.3	StarLAN
ring	802.5	token ring, ARCnet, FDDI
dual ring	802.6 (DQDB)	MAN

Unlike a telephone or computer network, LANs have flat structure that is optimized for device-to-device communication. This is in contrast to hierarchical networks where, for one device to talk to another, the message must traverse the host computer. LANs provide peer-to-peer or client/server computing by means of direct bus, ring, and star connections (Table 4.1). Each has strengths and weaknesses.

Bus and ring cost efficiencies have made them the dominant LAN topologies. The benefit that the ring offers for route redundancy has made it the favorite for broadband network implementation.

4.2.2. Access

LANs employ contention-based and deterministic access methods.

- For contention-based LANs such as Ethernet, all stations contend for available bandwidth on a first-come, first-served basis. If two or more stations access the LAN at the same time, a 'collision' occurs. Whenever a collision is detected, all stations back off and try to gain access to the bus at staggered intervals (Figure 4.3).
- Token ring employs a deterministic method of access. Each station is allocated a time interval during which it is guaranteed access to the shared ring. The time to transmit is controlled by a continuously circulating 'token'. When a terminal needs to transmit, it replaces the token with packets of data. After the transmission is completed, the token is reinserted, allowing another terminal to transmit.

4.2.3. Interface and Media

Ethernet LAN devices attach to the bus by means of a network interface card (NIC) that inserts into a computer or peripheral device. The NIC

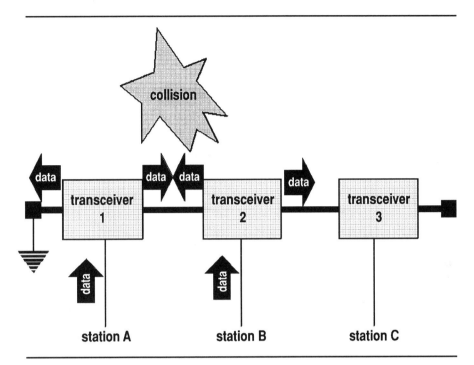

Figure 4.3.   Ethernet collision.

cable attaches to a transceiver, which plugs into the bus cable. For token ring, the connection is made with an adapter card that is inserted into each computer and peripheral device. The adapter cables to the media access unit (MAU), which plugs into the ring cable. LANs operate over a variety of media, ranging from voice-grade twisted-pair wiring to fiber cable to radio waves. The anticipated data rate determines the media. Early LANs used thick co-axial cabling that was inflexible and difficult to install. Later, more flexible thin co-axial cabling was introduced, and lower cost, shielded and unshielded twisted-pair wiring followed. Twisted-pair wiring already exists in most office environments. Backbone LANs with data rates of 100 Mb/s use fiber optic cabling. Fiber optic cable also improves immunity against electromechanical interference (EMI) and radio frequency interference (RFI). Wireless LANs use radio waves to connect terminals on the same floor of a building. Although wireless LANs are not as secure, security is improved by means of spread-spectrum transmission and encryption algorithms. The removal of media constraints has catapulted wireless LANs to popularity. A recent study projected that the wireless LAN market will increase by about 250% over the next three years (Table 4.2).

4.2.4. Protocols

LANs employ simple protocols that are inexpensive to implement, but work over limited distances. They differ from WAN protocols such as X.25 because they lack the extensive error protection required for long-distance transmission over noisy copper lines. The vastly increased

Table 4.2.   Wireless LAN market projection.

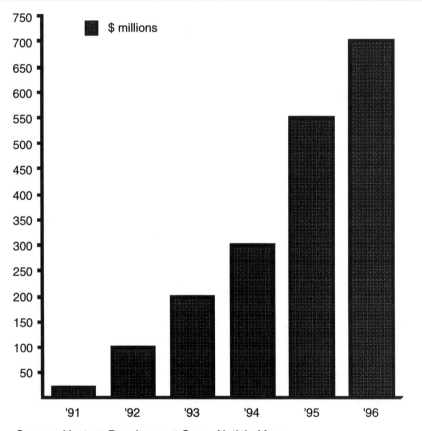

Source: Venture Development Corp., Natick, Mass.

amount of relatively noiseless fiber cable installed over the past decade in the public telephone network, and increased intelligence in the end-user terminals, have allowed these simpler protocols to migrate into the WAN. Any base-layer LAN protocol can be replaced by another without the user being aware of it. What does change is the LAN performance, particularly when one goes from the prevailing twisted-pair to fiber optic media (Table 4.3). With LANs, performance is measured in both speed and cost.

4.2.5. Network Management

The interface that the user sees and the number of users that share the network at the same time are governed by the manager. LAN network management is more than just provisioning and maintenance. These systems incorporate security and data protection, as well as databases for resource accounting and services such as E-mail. The management system uses software agents that reside in each device on the LAN. Instructions are communicated to individual devices from a central network management station. When LANs were separate islands of computing power, there was no need for the scope of the management station to extend beyond the LAN in which it resided. Modern LAN internets require that the manager control remote devices on other LANs. Moreover, each LAN can have its own local manager and yet be subservi-

Table 4.3.   LAN protocol performance.

Technology	Stated bandwidth (Mb/s)	Real bandwidth (Mb/s)	PC card cost (relative)	Media cost (relative)
Ethernet	10	1.5 to 3.0	low	medium
token ring	16	11 to 13	medium	medium
FDDI	100	70 to 80	high	high
FOIRL	10	1.5 to 3.0	medium	high
Fast ethernet (proposed)	100	15 to 30	medium	medium
ARCNET	2.5	1.7 to 2	low	medium
LocalTalk	0.25	0.04 to 0.08	no charge	low

ent to a remotely located management station. The situation is made even more complicated by the existence of other types of management systems, such as mainframe and WAN. The need to work in a hierarchical management environment has created the need for standardized ways to handle fault, security, configuration, performance, and device management. Various managements and tools include:

- Fault management tools, which identify a network problem with little or no human intervention. These tools forward alarms to other devices in the network or to the network administrator. Sophisticated tools have the ability to learn from prior faults. When a fault occurs, a database is searched so possible solutions can be forwarded with the alarm.
- Configuration management, which deals with the physical network properties. These tools identify each network element such as bridge, router, terminal, etc. This information is stored in the network database that is used to construct a map of the network topology with all its elements.
- Security management tools, which ensure system integrity. Some tools can configure a single address that receives or transmits data at the port level. When another address tries to communicate through this port, it will automatically be partitioned or blocked from entering the network. This allows the creation of secure subnetworks that protect the integrity of confidential information.
- Performance management tools, which allow network statistics to be viewed and collected. Alarms are generated when performance falls outside established limits.
- Element management protocols, such as simple network management protocol (SNMP), which allow disparate devices and management systems to communicate. SNMP is the most widely used way to gather and manage information, and can read an index of register values within a network device and change them, if required. Associated with SNMP are a number of management information bases (MIBs) that give a standard meaning to the values. Over time, several values have developed a standard meaning, but special functionality is still handled by proprietary MIB extensions.

Distributed management is particularly important on broadband LANs and internets where there may be thousands of users. The resulting information is valuable to staff at all levels in an enterprise. Some might want to monitor alarms and trouble tickets. A distributed management system allows them to be forwarded to all clients and servers that request such information, keeping everyone up to date. A critical alarm, for example, could be passed from the alarm collection server to the trouble ticket database server. There a problem record is created and propagated throughout the network.

Although the management of heterogenous LANs requires sophisticated systems, the broadband LAN itself is a relatively simple network.

4.3.   BROADBAND LANS

LAN architecture may be separated into two parts: the media access control (MAC) and the logical link control (LLC) sublayers of the OSI data link and physical layers (Figure 4.4). The MAC sublayer specifies how a device transmits and controls the signal over transmission media ranging from co-axial cable, twisted-pair wiring, fiber, and radio frequency. A variety of medium-dependent access control methods are standardized by the IEEE, including carrier sense multiple access with collision detection (CSMA/CD), token ring, and FDDI. The upper sublayer, logical link control (LLC), adds the routing capability to the data link layer. In this respect, the IEEE standard differs from the CCITT-approved OSI model. The OSI model relegates routing to layers 3 and 4. The transport of frames, like packet switching, requires some form of addressing to distinguish which data belongs to individual users. Connectionless and connection-oriented routing is possible with the LLC, which establishes connection, transfers data, and terminates connections. There are three ways that LANs route information:

- Unacknowledged connectionless service: For transport within the LAN there is no logical connection between source and destination. The frames are delivered on a best-effort basis, employing datagram service. Delivery is not guaranteed and lost frames are simply dropped, requiring the receiving device to request that the frames be retransmitted.
- Connection mode service: For interconnecting LANs, a logical connection between source and destination is established prior to transmission. This improves the efficiency of lengthy exchanges while relieving higher-level protocols from the burden of connection management.
- Acknowledged connectionless service: This is used for specialized applications such as point-of-sale or factory assembly where a large number of limited intelligence devices may communicate with a central processor. Frame receipt is acknowledged by the data link layer.

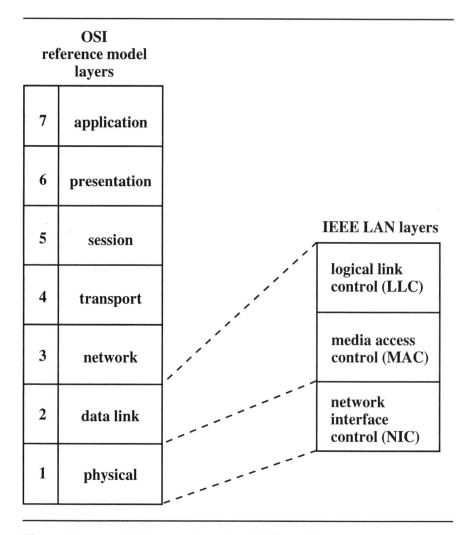

Figure 4.4. IEEE standards relation to OSI model.

By avoiding the processing overhead incurred by higher layer functions, LAN protocols are fast and relatively easy to implement.

The architecture of the LAN has always been vastly different from that of the WAN. First, the LAN uses protocols that would not work over the long distances associated with the WAN. These protocols give the LAN its broadband attributes, while maintaining a low-cost medium to interconnecting computers. In contrast, WAN communications protocols assure that information is protected from errors during transmission. The media employed by LANs also differs. Finally, the nature of the transported traffic differs; LANs were developed to transport data, WANs to transport voice. Thus the standards, equipment and functions of the two types of networks are so different that people think of them as separate entities.

With the increasing importance of broadband communications, these differences are being revisited. After all, the LAN is the most successful form of broadband network. Inherent features of the LAN such as frame-level communications are being adopted by the newer WAN technologies such as frame relay. And computer-derived technologies such as ATM, initially developed for the WAN, are entering LANs.

LANs come in many forms and varieties. This chapter concentrates on some standard ones; Ethernet, token ring, and FDDI (Figure 4.5).

4.3.1. Ethernet

With millions of networks in place, Ethernet is the most widely deployed LAN based on a bus topology (Figure 4.6). Alone, Ethernet accounts for over 45% of the installed LAN nodes. In the early 1970s, Ethernet was promoted by a coalition of DEC, Intel and Xerox. Xerox was the inventor, DEC the market provider, and Intel the silicon integrated circuit supplier. Ethernet allows all computers on the network equal access to the linear bus. Information transported by Ethernet is reduced to relatively small frames that include source and destination addresses as well as error protection mechanisms. The architecture was designed to transfer data at 10 Mb/s, maintaining simplicity and low cost. Trade-offs in the way that collisions are detected and traffic controlled limit the distance over which the protocols are effective.

The access method, CSMA/CD, regulates how terminals share the common bus. The probability that a collision will occur depends on the number of terminals on the LAN. The more terminals, the greater the number of collisions. Each terminal 'listens' to determine if the bus is idle before transmitting its frame. If several terminals attempt to transmit at the same time, a collision results. The data gets distorted. This condition is resolved by having the terminals release the bus and reconnect at staggered intervals. Some applications cannot tolerate the lengthy delays that occur with CSMA/CD. Another source of delay is the way that traffic volume is controlled. When there is too much traffic for a receiving device, the device simply discards the message. Since messages are numbered and the transmitting device waits for an ac-

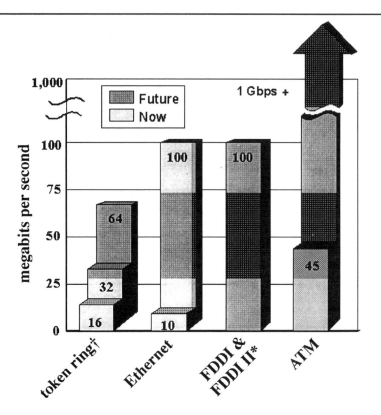

† Two future speeds have been developed
* No increase is expected
Source: Communication Week

Figure 4.5.   Current and potential future speeds of various LAN types.

knowledgment, discarded messages can be detected and retransmitted, but this substantially degrades performance.

Ethernet uses three types of cables; thin co-ax, thick co-ax, and unshielded-twisted pair—referred to as 10BASE2, 10BASE5 and 10BASE-T, respectively. The most recent standard, 10BASE-T, works with existing telephone wiring systems. The use of CSMA/CD imposes a practical limit on the length of the bus. The IEEE 802.3 Ethernet standard allows 500-meter cable lengths without repeaters for signal regeneration. Repeaters extend the bus to 2500 meters—approximately

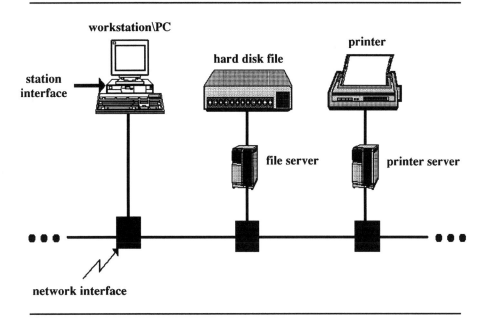

workstation\PC

printer

hard disk file

station
interface

file server

printer server

network interface

Figure 4.6.   Ethernet local area network.

2.5 miles. A maximum of four repeater units may be in the signal path between any two stations on the network. While repeaters amplify and reconstitute weak signals, they do not compensate for signal propagation delays. Unless distance limits are observed, signal delays may become so great that the terminal at the end of the bus may not detect that another terminal is transmitting.

4.3.1.1. Frame.   A data stream represents a pattern of binary bits. With Ethernet, this stream is transported in the form of frames (Figure 4.7). That is, data are encapsulated in an IEEE 802.3 standardized format called a *frame* that is recognized by any Ethernet adaptor. The frame contains addressing, routing, and error checking information as well as the following data fields:

- Preamble field: Each frame begins with an eight-byte preamble field. Seven bytes are used for synchronization and to define the frame. The remaining byte indicates where the frame begins.
- Address Field: The address field consists of destination and source addresses. The destination address field identifies the location of

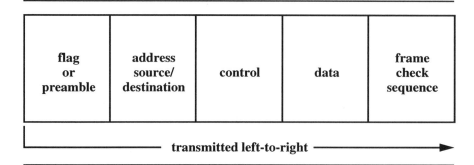

Figure 4.7. Generic IEEE LAN frame.

the receiving terminal. The source address field identifies the sending station. The address field can be either two bytes (16-bits) or six bytes (48-bits) in length. A destination address can refer to one terminal, a specific group of terminals, or all terminals.

- Control Field: The Ethernet control field indicates the length of the data field and provides padding for detecting collisions. The length of the data field is indicated by the two-byte length count field. This field determines the length of the data unit when a pad field is included in the frame. Padding is used for collision detection. A frame must contain a specified number of bytes. If a frame does not meet this minimum length, bits are added.

- Data Field: Transported information is encapsulated in the data field in the form of eight-bit bytes. The minimum frame size is 72 bytes, the maximum is 1526 bytes. The maximum frame size reflects practical considerations related to adapter card buffer sizes and the need to limit the length of time the medium is tied up in transmitting a single frame. If the data to be sent exceeds 1526 bytes, the higher layers break it into individual packets in a procedure called *fragmentation*.

- Frame Check Sequence: The frame check sequence terminates the frame. It has two purposes; to define the end of the frame, and to check for errors. Both the sending and receiving terminals perform cyclical redundancy checks on the frame bits. The sending terminal stores the result of this calculation in the four-byte frame check sequence field. The receiving terminal compares the cyclical redundancy checks that it calculates with this value. If the two numbers do not match, a transmission error has occurred and the frame is retransmitted.

4.3.1.2. Network Addresses.   One reason for the popularity of IEEE-standard LANs is the unique address given to every device that connects to the LAN. Ethernet supports universal and network-specific addresses. Manufacturers of Ethernet NICs are granted address space that they alone can use, insuring that every Ethernet device has a unique and identifiable address no matter were it is located.[3] Thus network interconnection devices such as bridges can automatically route Ethernet frames based on the existence of a unique address for the receiving terminal. Whether universal or network-specific, the address can be set by the terminal itself during initialization. Any frame sent to this address is received and processed by the terminal. With universal addressing, all devices on the network have unique addresses. With network-specific addressing, each terminal is given an address that is unique within the network, but which can be the same as a terminal on another network. Because Ethernet does not specify how the 48 bits of an address must be used, network-specific addressing is possible. In this case, when networks are interconnected, a unique network identifier is attached to the terminal address to provide a unique address.

Ethernet also supports the use of multicast and broadcast addresses. An address consisting of all '1' bits is defined as the broadcast address and is received by all terminals. An address associated with a particular group of stations is a multicast address. A multicast address is identified by the value '1' in the first bit of the address. Individual terminals can be enabled for multicast, allowing terminals to accept frames with multicast addresses.

4.3.1.3. Physical Elements.   Ethernet defines the electrical and mechanical characteristics below that enable components from different vendors to be interconnected.

* Physical configuration: This defines limits, cable length, number of repeaters, total path length, and transceiver cable length. The most common Ethernet architecture, 10BASE-5, uses baseband transmission over co-axial cable at a data rate of 10 Mb/s. The maximum cable length is 500 meters.
* Co-axial cable specifications: This includes the cabling, connectors and terminators. 10BASE-5 installations use a relatively expensive 50-ohm co-axial cable with a diameter of 10 mm, now referred to as

---

[3]The maximum source or destination address is 2^{48}.

'thick Ethernet cable'. Another cable standard, 10BASE-2 (meaning 10 Mb/s, baseband signaling, 200 meters), uses ordinary CATV-type co-axial cable, called 'thin Ethernet cable'. Twisted-pair wiring has emerged as an alternative under the 10BASE-T standard.

- Transceiver specifications: This includes the cable as well as the transceiver. The migration from thick co-axial cable to thin Ethernet ('Cheapernet') to telephone twisted-pair wiring increases the complexity of the transceiver, but saves in both installation and cable costs.
- Environmental specifications.

Ethernet has demonstrated a surprising ability to adapt to market demands for greater economy and speed. Some vendors have suggested increasing Ethernet's 10 Mb/s capacity with an extension to existing standards; others want to boost the performance of existing Ethernet LANs through proprietary methods.

4.3.2.   Fast Ethernet

Ethernet performance is limited in several ways. First, the data rate and contention protocols do not support voice traffic. Second, a shared-media LAN limits the amount of bandwidth available for specific applications. As more users are added, each receives a smaller percentage of the total bandwidth. The rate at which a single device—server, personal computer, or workstation—can transmit and receive from the network is limited because they all share access to the bus. For example, if a LAN has two servers, each with the capability of transmitting at the full Ethernet bandwidth, the throughput of each server is halved.

Conventional Ethernet transmits data at 10 Mb/s. The emerging Fast Ethernet can accommodate transmissions of up to 100 Mb/s. The IEEE 802.3 committee has already begun work on a standard for fast Ethernet to bring high-speed communications to the desktop. This standard will allow users to develop new applications for videoconferencing, graphics, voice processing, and other technologies.

Ethernet popularity stems from its economical connectivity. Fast Ethernet follows this tradition. The key ingredient of fast Ethernet is the use of existing copper wiring instead of fiber optic cabling. The IEEE committee wants the standard to operate over ordinary voice-grade unshielded twisted-pair copper wiring so users will not have to rewire. A number of problems must be resolved first though. Foremost among them is the format of the standard.

Fast Ethernet, like traditional 10 Mb/s Ethernet, uses the MAC layer and the physical, or signaling, layer. For the physical layer, one proposal uses the American National Standards Institute (ANSI) X3T9.5 physical medium-dependent (PMD) sublayer, and the existing Ethernet MAC. This physical layer is mated to a 100 Mb/s Ethernet (CSMA/CD) MAC with a translating function called 100BASE-X. Preserving Ethernet's core specification, the CSMA/CD MAC would significantly reduce the time to standardization. Using an unchanged CSMA/CD MAC for fast Ethernet is supported by Grand Junction Networks, Inc., LAN Media Corp., Sun Microsystems, SynOptics, and 3Com, among others.

Another proposal, 100BASE-VG, supported by AT&T and Hewlett-Packard, replaces the CSMA/CD with a new access method called demand priority, in which a station requests permission to transmit data at a specific level of priority. A concentrator module grants permission to transmit data and directs the incoming data to the appropriate destination. If multiple transmissions occur at once, the higher-priority requests are serviced first. The demand protocol can supply guaranteed bandwidth and priority of service, two attributes critical for multimedia networking. Guaranteed bandwidth is also important for scaleability because under the current 10 Mb/s Ethernet standard, the performance of the LAN declines as more users are added. With the demand protocol, the performance of the network is bounded by the speed of the concentrator module. Is it Ethernet? The standards committee will have to overcome resistance to this radical departure from the current Ethernet standard.

4.3.3. Token Ring

Token ring is a token passing network that operates at four or 16 Mb/s (Figure 4.8). Information exchange occurs via a token that is circulated around the ring. Each terminal, in sequence, is given a chance to put information on the network. When a terminal accepts the token, the token is replaced with a frame containing data. The destination terminal retains the message, and only the station that put the message on the ring can remove it. The maximum amount of time that a terminal occupies the network before passing the token to another terminal is determined by a token holding timer. Because each terminal regenerates the token back to the original signal strength, ring LANs support greater distance and speed than bus LANs. Ring networks also provide flow control, which is implemented with a 'refuse bit' near the end of the message. The receiving terminal can leave this bit set, indicating to the transmitter that the message was not accepted.

The ring topology has been reserved for LANs in which users are

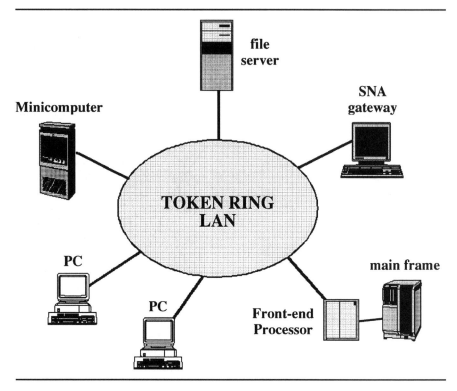

Figure 4.8. Token ring LAN.

not concerned about the cost of duplicate lines. Now this topology is migrating to broadband WANs as those users appreciate the ring's advantages:

- Higher data rates.
- Fewer routing problems (messages may be broadcast to selected nodes).
- Simplified control (little in the way of additional hardware or software is needed).
- Improved reliability (because of redundant paths).
- High priority traffic can be granted preference (a priority indicator is embedded in the token).

Specific procedures such as *neighbor notification* ensure that new terminals are recognized by others and granted a proportionate share of network time. Upon power-up, each station becomes acquainted with the address of its neighbors on the network. Addresses are periodically re-broadcast thereafter. A special frame is broadcast to all stations on a ring. The first terminal downstream of the broadcaster will recognize that certain bits within the frame are zero. This terminal has now learned the address of its nearest neighbor, and resets some of these bits to 1 so terminals further downstream will not see all the bits as zero. This process continues in daisy chain fashion until every station knows the identity of its upstream neighbor. This knowledge is important in case of a ring failure. When a hard failure occurs because of a broken cable, jabbering station, or failed PC adapter card, among other reasons, its cause is isolated by the upstream station, which reports a failure by transmitting beacon MAC frames.

Token ring LANs are not without problems. Failed nodes and links can break the ring, preventing all other terminals from using the network unless a dual ring configuration with redundant hardware and bypass circuitry is used to isolate faulty nodes from the rest of the network. With bypass circuitry, physically adding or deleting terminals from the token ring network is accomplished without breaking the ring. Token rings are also vulnerable to terminal failures that occur before the terminal passes the token. The network is down until a new token is inserted. The token may also become corrupted to the point of being unrecognizable to the terminals. When this occurs, a token time out alerts all stations on the ring that the token protocol has been suspended. The network can also be disrupted by the occasional appearance of two tokens, or by the presence of a continuously circulating data packet, which can happen when data is sent to a failed terminal, and the originating terminal gets disabled before it can remove the packet from the ring. These failures require more sophisticated recovery mechanisms.

To protect the token ring from potential disaster, one terminal is typically designated as the control station. This terminal supervises network operations and does important housecleaning chores, such as reinserting lost tokens, taking extra tokens off the network, and disposing of 'lost' packets. To guard against the failure of the control station, every station is equipped with control circuitry so the first station detecting the failure of the control station assumes responsibility for network supervision. A variation of token-passing allows devices to send data only during specified time intervals. The ability to determine the time interval between messages is a major advantage over CSMA access methods. Since each device transmits only during a small percentage of the total available time, no one station uses the full capacity of the network. This time slot approach can support voice transmission and may be employed more frequently as token ring LANs adopt 100 Mb/s data rates.

4.4.   THE FIBER DISTRIBUTED DATA INTERFACE (FDDI)

FDDI is a high-performance, 100 Mb/s backbone LAN supporting high-powered workstations and slower local area data networks (Figure 4.9)—the first truly broadband LAN. There are thousands of FDDI LANs installed, and ANSI and OSI standards are well developed. The ANSI standard for FDDI defines two parallel, timed token-passing rings, one active and the other in backup for a secure physical link. An FDDI LAN can support up to 1000 physical connections over distances of 200 kilometers. Originally, the FDDI standard specified the use of multimode fiber, which limited the maximum distance between two nodes to 2 kilometers. Use of single-mode fiber has extended this distance to up to 40 kilometers (Table 4.4). Thus, FDDI stretches over greater distances and provides higher bandwidths than Ethernet or the token ring LANs, providing a solution for leading-edge applications such as:

- Archiving: FDDI can minimize the time required to back up files.
- Network backbone: Low-speed LANs may be joined using an FDDI LAN. For Ethernet, this provides ten times the bandwidth.

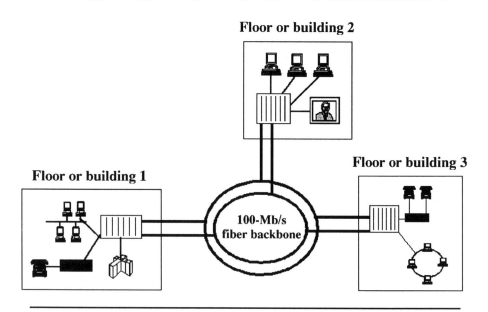

Figure 4.9.   FDDI merges data, video and voice.

Table 4.4. FDDI Media vs. Distance.

Media	Distance
Multimode fiber	up to 2 Km
Singlemode fiber	up to 40 Km
Twisted-pair copper (TWP–150 ohm)	up to 100 meters
Unshielded twisted-pair (UTP–100ohm)	less than 100 meters
Thin-wire coaxial cable (RG58–50 ohm)	up to 100 meters

- Computer room networks: An FDDI LAN may locally connect high speed computers.
- High-speed LAN: An FDDI wiring hub may be connected in a star configuration to FDDI-equipped computer workstations.
- CAD/CAM: Large CAD/CAM images can be transported, allowing instantaneous sharing of files between multiple stations.
- File servers: File servers can be connected directly to an FDDI backbone, speeding the flow of information.
- Image processing: Real-time access to large graphics files makes image processing applications such as medical imaging a reality.

4.4.1. Operation

FDDI uses a token-passing access method—similar to token ring LANs—over two counter-rotating optical fiber rings. One ring is set up as the primary ring, the other is a backup. The dual-ring topology provides redundancy: if there is a failure on the primary ring, the backup ring automatically begins transporting traffic. On an FDDI ring, stations attached to both rings are called dual access stations (DASs) and stations attached to just one ring are called single access stations (SASs). Links between SAS nodes are not self-healing since there is only one ring between them. FDDI allocates bandwidth both asynchronously and synchronously. Synchronous transmission allows continuous, fixed data-rate conversations. Asynchronous dialogs allow two terminals to keep the token and exchange data between themselves for extended periods.

The four key components of FDDI are:

- Physical layer medium dependent (PMD): At the lowest level, the PMD handles the electronic transition. It converts optical signals from the fiber into electronic pulses and passes the bit information to the physical layer.

- Physical protocol at the physical layer: Timing and encoding take place in the physical layer.
- Media access control (MAC) at the data link layer: The MAC layer assembles bits into frames that are handed to the network via IEEE 802.2 logical link control (LLC).
- Station management transcending both layers (SMT): The SMT allows FDDI stations to communicate with each other for connection, configuration, and fault management.

SMT also defines the Management Information Base (MIB) in each station, which includes a set of managed objects and their attributes. A MIB might contain the number of ports in the station, its current configuration, and statistics such as the number of frame errors. The SMT software also defines operations that can be performed on managed objects, and how events and conditions are handled. Although FDDI is significantly more expensive than Ethernet or token ring, the costs may be justified by its increased speed, reduced downtime, and fewer backbone congestion problems. Moreover, its network management features are built-in. Therefore, changes in configuration are implemented transparently to the user, providing a fault-tolerant and self-healing system (Figure 4.10).

There are variations of FDDI that lower installation and operating costs. For example, copper distributed data interface (CDDI) uses copper wire rather than fiber optic cable. While reducing costs, CDDI is not widely deployed because of limitations including: shorter distances between stations (100 meters or less); susceptibility to electromagnetic interference (from sources such as electrical motors); and fiber optic DAS connections needed for network redundancy. Other FDDI extensions transport voice as well as data.

4.4.2. Voice on FDDI-II

FDDI transmits data frames but does not guarantee when the frames will be delivered. Voice transmission requires an isochronous transport capable of guaranteeing access to the network at specified time frames. Using an isochronous service is like making a telephone call: one makes a reservation for the length of the call and the amount of bandwidth that is needed. Connection delays are small enough so that data and voice transport can be transported together.

To support isochronous transmission, FDDI-II extends the FDDI

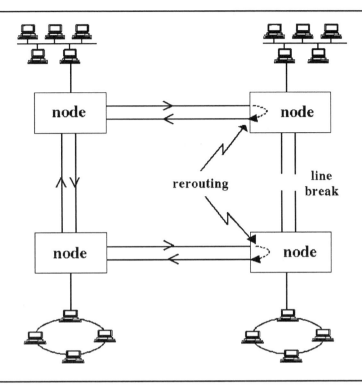

Figure 4.10. FDDI self-healing.

specification with an overlay of synchronous services. Connections between nodes can be made for guaranteed duration and data rates. FDDI-
II uses updated versions of MAC and the physical layer known as
MAC-2 and PHY-2. An expanded version of the SMT, SMT-2, includes
the services needed to support isochronous circuit switching simultaneously with packet switching. A new function—hybrid ring control
(HRC)—handles circuit and frame switching.

FDDI-II uses up to sixteen 6.144 Mb/s channels that may be subdivided into a number of transmission channels of varying bandwidth,
depending on the services to be provided. ISDN, for example, has each
channel defined as an increment of 64 kb/s, making the frame size
convenient for connection to the public ISDN network. The 16 channels
use 98.3 Mb/s of the 100 Mb/s bandwidth. The remaining bandwidth is
divided among a 768 kb/s packet-switched channel, and 928 kb/s is used
for management overhead. The bandwidth of each of the 16 FDD-II

channels is further divided into bytes of data that are spaced within 96 groups per 125 microsecond intervals. These small bytes of bandwidth ensure the predictable transmission of voice and video applications.

4.4.3. LocalTalk

LocalTalk ports come standard with all Apple Macintosh computers and Apple Finder operating systems. Its claim to fame, other than its Apple connection, is simplicity—there is almost no setup. LocalTalk employs standard twisted-pair (STP) wiring and has a maximum data rate of 230 kb/s. Like Ethernet, it is a multiple-access method, although it employs Carrier Sense, Multiple Access with Collision Avoidance (CSMA/CA), which differs from Ethernet's CSMA/CD because its emphasis is on collision avoidance, not detection.

4.4.4. ARCNET

ARCNET began as a 2.5 Mb/s local network promoted by Datapoint in 1977. Today it reaches speeds of 20 Mb/s. ARCNET is organized as a logical ring and uses token-passing access. The identifications of individual terminals are physically set by an administrator, and an auto reconfiguration sequence is required if the network connections change. While it has a loyal following, its popularity is limited because Datapoint kept ARCNET proprietary, allowing Ethernet and token ring to proliferate.

4.5.   CONCLUSION

There is no aspect of computing that is more competitive than the local environment. LANs have always been broadband and continue to evolve at an accelerating pace; almost before the ink dries on one standard, another rises. (Witness the battle between vendor proponents of Fast Ethernet.) Another 100 Mb/s LAN, FDDI, has been available for several years and is evolving toward lower-cost data as well as voice connectivity. Several things are clear: the relatively low-cost, open connectivity LANs offer will continue to attract users and new, powerful LAN networking technologies, and topologies will enter the public telephone network in the guise of broadband WANs.

5

LAN Internetworking

5.1. INTRODUCTION

LAN internetworks employ a variety of networking elements. Some, like the hub, evolved from intra-LAN applications. Others, like the bridge, router, and gateway were specifically intended for internetworks. All are evolving toward increasing function and performance. Industry experts foresee a time when the same technology will be used from the desktop to the LAN and throughout the enterprise WAN. One consequence of that will be the disappearance of the distinction between LANs and WANs because the same protocols and transmission rates will be used. Voice, data, and video will be seamlessly transported across private and public networks.

5.2. PRIVATE NETWORKS

The past decade has seen unprecedented growth in private corporate networks, growth fueled by favorable tariffs and technology. LANs have become a strategic part of the organizational infrastructure, providing distributed processing and increased user productivity. The sophistication of local networks in managing heterogeneous environments has, in many respects, exceeded that of the public telephone network. But the need for even higher data rates on LANs, and the need to interconnect LANs over public networks, has created a crisis in networking. Its resolution requires a radical departure from the constraints of shared-media LANs.

Networks based on emerging technologies such as ATM work differently. ATM is not a connectionless LAN protocol, it is a connection-oriented network technology. It supports hierarchical, unique station addresses that are similar to telephone numbers. These create connections between premises switches and carrier switches just as the public telephone network links private branch exchanges (PBXs) and central office switches (COs). ATM will enable switched LANs. When these LANs are connected to WANs, they will form the basis of the first truly universal virtual network. For many firms, considerations such as price, interoperability, and network management will be key criteria in purchasing ATM products and services. They look to ATM to provide *one* on-site interface technology that integrates text, images, voice, and video. The public carriers have the opportunity to satisfy these needs and, in the process, bring the private networks back into the public fold.

There is also the arrival of LAN network elements in the internetworking fray to consider. How quickly these devices evolve into true internetworking vehicles will determine whether it is the public telephone carriers or private networks that win the battle to service the broadband communications needs of modern businesses.

5.3.   LAN INTERNETS

As LANs have proliferated, it has become increasingly necessary to connect them. This may be done locally—in a single building, perhaps—by means of a backbone LAN. More common is the use of a WAN to connect dispersed LANs, forming an integrated enterprise network. The devices that remove the distance limitations of LANs span the layers of the OSI reference model (Table 5.1). A LAN internet is formed from individual LANs that are connected by means of repeaters (OSI model layer 1), bridges (OSI model layer 2), or routers (OSI model layer 3) to a network. The network may be a backbone LAN such as FDDI, an extended LAN (referred to as a metropolitan area network, or MAN), or a WAN.

5.3.1. Repeaters

Repeaters are the simplest devices used to interconnect LANs. They do not control or route information, nor do they generally have management capabilities. Repeaters work at the physical layer of the OSI model and ignore higher-layer protocols while regenerating signals to extend the distance they can travel *and* remain recognizable to the receiving device. Repeaters extend the network because the distance a single LAN

Table 5.1.   LAN Interconnection Devices.

OSI layer	Device	Function
7 Application		
6 Presentation	Gateway	Connects different protocols
5 Session		
4 Transport		
3 Network	Router	Acknowledgement messages, sequence numbers and flow control
2 Data Link	Bridge	Divides a network into separate segments, ignoring the network protocol. Provides traffic balance by filtering traffic within local segments.
1 Physical	Repeater	Transfers the digital data bit–for–bit, ignoring any format or protocol. Used for increasing distance between source and destination.

may span is limited by signal distortion. When signals become too distorted, their information is lost. There is no isolation between LAN segments connected by a repeater, so a single, extended LAN is created. Where repeaters are effective—in addition to extending signal distance—is in linking different types of network media; thick/thin co-axial cable, copper twisted-pair, fiber, etc. LANs that employ different media are often interconnected in a campus environment by means of repeaters.

There are limits to the use of repeaters. Ethernet, for example, limits the number of repeaters to four. More intelligent network elements—gateways, routers, and bridges—extend the LAN even further.

5.3.2. Gateway

A gateway works at OSI layer four and above to convert disparate protocols and network operating systems. For example, a gateway providing access from a personal computer to an IBM mainframe would convert between the LAN and systems network architecture (SNA) protocol environment. Gateways are often used to make E-mail systems communicate with other sites and organizations. An E-mail gateway's function is to leave messages intact by translating address headers between different mail systems. E-mail gateways that internetwork among different systems provide a common denominator between those systems, with each system providing its own gateway to the common backbone protocol. The most common E-mail gateways are to simple mail transfer protocol (SMTP) and to X.400. SMTP, the Unix/Internet E-mail protocol, is important because it is the Internet protocol. X.400, the CCITT-standard E-mail protocol, is important because it is the most comprehensive of all E-mail addressing protocols. Today, X.400 serves as a backbone transport solution for other types of E-mail applications. The migration from a messaging pipe to an all-encompassing messaging environment requires satisfying customer concerns about interoperability and directory services.

Interoperability concerns are about mail systems from different vendors such as Lotus and Microsoft as well as different X.400 versions. The 1984 version of X.400 contains basic specifications for E-mail system interconnection and the 1988 version extends this to encompass guidelines for distribution lists, large messages, and file attachments for various data types. This is compatible with another OSI standard: X.500 directory services. The evolving X.500 standard outlines a way to build a common resource directory for different networks which makes it much easier to find address information or X.400 interconnected networks.

Because of the extensive amount of processing required for this level of protocol conversion, the gateway is the slowest device used to interconnect LANs. Despite the increase in computer power, which speeds the processing of complex protocols, the gateway has given way to faster routers and bridges that do the interconnection but relegate protocol conversions to the connecting device.

5.3.3. Routers

Routers are today's backbone internetworking device. Within the LAN, there are no dedicated paths between sending and receiving devices. To send a message, one broadcasts it to all nodes. The receiving router separates the messages (Figure 5.1). This is referred to as a *connectionless protocol*. Each device on the LAN reads the address of the message, accepts those addressed to it, and either forwards or ignores other messages. The router acts for devices on other LANs by intercepting messages and forwarding them to remote locations.

As networks grow, they are often divided into more manageable segments. Also, as internetworks are formed, networks are formed. Therein lies the problem of individual networks employing different

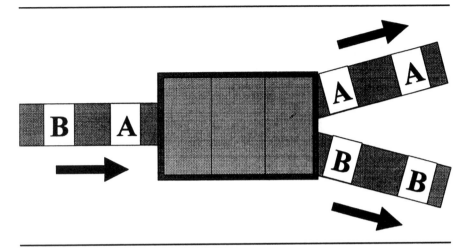

Figure 5.1.   Message addressing schemes.

protocols. Finally, there is the issue of alternate routes between networks to provide a more reliable internetwork. Routers perform these functions by interconnecting networks at OSI layer 3. The router is able to connect devices based on their logical address, which allows complex internetworks to be created. These networks can be potentially independent administrative domains because the router stores a map of the entire network it uses to determine the best path to a destination.

When a packet arrives at the router, it is stored until the router finishes handling the previous packet. If the packet is too large for the destination network to accept, the router segments it into several smaller packets. The router reads the destination address and looks it up in its routing table. The routing table lists the various nodes on the network, as well as the paths between the nodes and their associated costs. If there is more than one path to a particular node, the router selects the most economical path based on predetermined criteria. The logical addresses used by the router are not unique, and naming conventions must be carefully chosen to avoid duplication. But they allow device hierarchies where part of the address is assigned to a group of terminals designated as a network, subnetwork, or area, and where the remainder is used to designate the particular station in the network or subnetwork. One result of hierarchical addressing is that routers can store addressing information for networks with very large numbers of stations. Moreover, routers have detailed information about packet transmissions including the location of stations, packet lifetime, and paths between nodes, among other things. They use this information to select among alternate paths.

5.3.3.1. Routing Standards.   How information is transported across a network is not the concern of the user. Routing algorithms keep transmission detail hidden. Most algorithms automatically establish routes between network nodes from the source and destination addresses (Figure 5.2). An algorithm may employ static and dynamic routing. With static routing, the router contains a fixed routing table which contains preset routes. A dynamic router configures the routing table automatically. The routing table provides a dynamic record of a router's neighbors as well as where each device on the network is located. Upon receiving a packet of information, the router examines the source address and compares it to entries in its table. If the source address is not

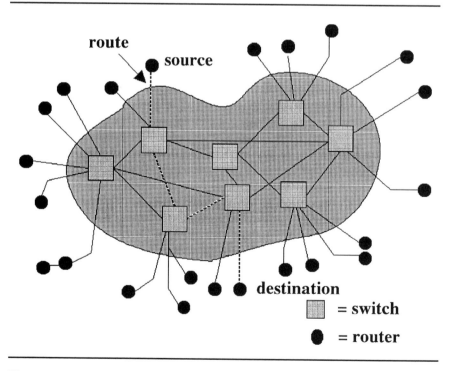

Figure 5.2.   Router paths.

in the table, the new address is added. Next, it reads the destination address and compares it with the addresses in the table. These routing algorithms and table update methods are incorporated in routing protocols. Various protocols exist at OSI layers 3 to 5, which exchange route and path information. Each network protocol has its own routing protocol, which can get confusing because acronyms may be the same, but have different meanings. Moreover, the protocols route in different ways. Two routing protocols employed in the transport control protocol/internet protocol (TCP/IP) internet are discussed in this section. Each has strengths and weaknesses.

5.3.3.2. Routing Information Protocol (RIP)[4]***.*** This routing method, often used in TCP/IP-based Internet, uses the TCP/IP gateway/gateway protocol (GGP). The number of routers encountered by a route setup or discovery packet as it travels from the source to destination devices determines the path. The route with the least number of routers wins. The individual routers retain routing tables that are periodically updated as each router sends a copy of its table to its neighbor. This occurs even when there are no changes, consuming valuable bandwidth. While this works well for smaller networks, it creates problems with larger networks for several reasons. Since routing is done irrespectively of significant factors such as delay and bandwidth, it is not always the best criteria for larger networks. As network size increases, routing updates limit the use of RIP to networks with less than 100 routers because the routing algorithm requires that the whole routing table be broadcast frequently throughout the network. When a failure occurs, this lengthy procedure slows the discovery of a new route.

5.3.3.3. Open Shortest Path First (OSPF). OSPF addresses these issues. With OSPF, distributed routing tables are constructed. Each router on the network broadcasts a packet that describes its local links to all other routers. These description packets are relatively small and consume relatively small amounts of bandwidth. Moreover, OSPF issues updates only when necessary, saving more bandwidth. Whenever a link fails, updated information floods the network, creating new routing tables. The table criteria include such factors as delay, bandwidth, and the dollar cost of the facility. For example, assume a packet can take one path that goes through two routers and another that goes

---

[4]This is a good example of the misuse of acronyms. TCP/IP RIP is not the same as the Novell Netware SPX/IPX RIP.

through three. RIP will always take the two-router path. In contrast, OSPF chooses a path based on criteria provided by the network manager that include line speed, cost and traffic loads. If there are multiple paths of equal weight, OSPF will balance the traffic load between them. Type-of-service routing allows the user to specify up to 16 classes of service and establish a separate path for each class. This, for example, allows the transmission of batch files over a long-delay, high-capacity satellite link, and the transmission of interactive 'bursty' traffic over short-delay, low-capacity terrestrial leased lines.

5.4.   BRIDGES

What separates bridges from routers is raw speed. A bridge can connect at the LAN wire speed, which, for Ethernet, exceeds 30,000 frames/ second. As LANs grow, the number of users may cause congestion. One way to alleviate congestion is to use a bridge to segment the LAN into separate parts. Architecturally, a network that is interconnected by bridging appears as a single logical network, while an inter-LAN network using routers appears as a connected group of separate networks. The bridge connects LANs at a relatively low level, the sublayer of the data link layer. It routes by means of the Logical Link Control (LLC), the upper sublayer of the data link layer. Logically the LAN is one, but the physical separation, if properly done, allows most traffic to remain within its segment, decreasing congestion. From this local application, bridges have evolved into full networking devices. In fact, some protocols such as the DEC LAT cannot be routed and must be bridged onto the internetwork.* Nonetheless, bridges remain true to their roots as data link layer devices that forward or block traffic, depending on the source, destination, and protocol information contained in the data-link layer frame.

Whereas routers operate on OSI level 3 and connect different hierarchies of networks, bridges operate at layer 2 and connect physical station addresses within the same network. Because there is no logical separation and physically independent LANs appear as a single network, the individual LAN segments must use compatible protocols, unless the bridge has a special frame translation capability—Ethernet to token ring, for example. Most networks that employ bridges adhere to IEEE stan-

---

*The LAT protocol allows a terminal server to connect multiple asynchronous devices—video display terminals, printers, etc.—to a host computer.

dards because these networks ensure that every device has a unique data link layer address.

Modern bridges are able to filter information, learn device locations, and perform a rudimentary form of routing, as detailed below:

• Filtering: Filtering is performed by means of the frame address and control fields. The bridge reads the individual frames on one LAN subnetwork and routes only the frames between subnetworks that have the proper addresses or control field.

• Learning: An intelligent bridge is capable of learning the locations of all devices on the LAN. The frames of IEEE LANs contain devices' addresses that are assigned by the IEEE to the manufacturers of LAN-attachment devices.

• Routing: Bridges employ routing algorithms such as *transparent spanning tree* and *source routing* that allow them to link LANs transparently at remote locations. Transparent bridges, using the IEEE spanning-tree algorithm in the Ethernet environment, determine a path between local and remote LANs that does not loop back to its origin. In contrast, source routing, employed in token ring bridges, sends discovery frames to determine all possible routes between local and remote LANs. Since this process also determines the network topology, closed loops can be tolerated. The IEEE *transparent source routing* method works with either algorithm.

These algorithms differ from those employed by routers in the degree of sophistication of their interconnected network. The bridge algorithms form flat networks where all devices are equal, while the router is able to form network hierarchies, which allow routers to transport information more selectively. Routers can keep certain types of broadcast and multicast messages from entering the WAN and route others over a single path to the destination LAN.

5.5.   HUBS

Early LANs used a single, shared wire that all stations tapped into as needed. The cable weaved from office to office throughout a floor. A major problem with this approach was that a break in the cable could disable the entire LAN. The hub concept began as a way to remedy this situation. Initially, hubs were essentially multiple-port repeaters. These hubs received the signal over a wire that was terminated at a single location, preferably in a closet. Such hubs provided isolation between small segments of networked computers. If any segment failed, only the computers attached to that segment were affected. From this simple beginning, hubs have become central switches, embracing internetworking, switching, and multimedia. The flexibility of the hub accrues from its modular construction. Three basic components are used—chassis, backplane, and cards (Figure 5.3).

The chassis is the hub's most visible component. It contains several card slots and an integral power supply. The chassis usually has a high degree of redundancy in power and card connections, achieved by means of the hub backplane design. Some have separate channels that can simultaneously handle network types (LAN or WAN, for example). Others load-share, letting the cards select the channel that will transport the information. Still others are rigidly segmented, having specific channels for Ethernet, token ring, and FDDI, and a fast-packet bus for connecting the hub to the WAN. Whatever the current backplane design, it is its evolution that will make the hub an even more significant networking element in the future, allowing information to flow freely across network borders (Figure 5.4). The types of cards plugged into the chassis give the hub its personality. Individual cards can support different types of LANs and media, serve as internetworking devices, and provide intelligent management.

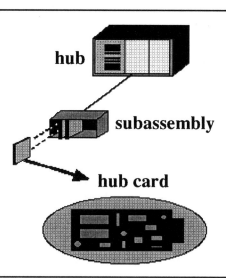

Figure 5.3. LAN hub construction.

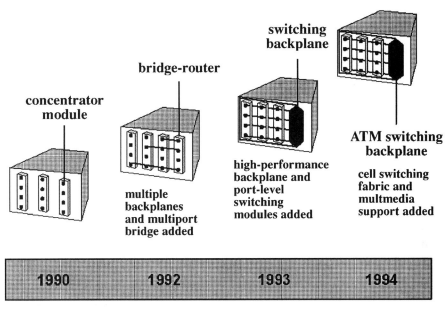

switching
backplane

bridge-router

concentrator
module

ATM switching
backplane

high-performance
backplane and
port-level
switching
modules added

cell switching
fabric and
multmedia
support added

multiple
backplanes
and multiport
bridge added

| 1990 | 1992 | 1993 | 1994 |

Source: Communications Week

Figure 5.4.   Hub evolution.

Nonetheless, the most important feature of the hub is its capability to alter topology. The hub's logical topology is different from the network's physical topology. This allows changes to the network layout—adding and deleting devices—without pulling cables. Wiring changes are done by management software, centralizing network maintenance. The hub concentrates a building-wide LAN's internetworking devices into a single controlled area, allowing troubleshooting from one location. From the hub, every device attached to the LAN or WAN can be controlled and analyzed. Moreover, the intelligent hub has a switching capability. There are five kinds of switching available on hubs: port, bank, card, Ethernet, and cell.

- Port Switching: An administrator can assign any given port in a card to any logical network.
- Bank Switching: The same as port switching, with the addition that any given port can be made part of a logical grouping of ports by the administrator.

- Card Switching: The network administrator can switch a bridge, router, or repeater card from one backplane bus to another to balance the traffic.
- Ethernet Switching: Individual Ethernet frames are switched based on the destination address. This treats the LAN as a PBX rather than a party line. Ethernet switching bypasses the CSMA/CD protocol used by Ethernet to deliver the full 10 Mb/s bandwidths to each port up to the bandwidth capacity of the hub. There are two switching designs; one sends the frame out to the destination port before it has arrived at the input port, the other relies on wire speed control of each frame.
- Cell Switching: A variant of ATM in which the data is segmented into 53-byte cells. The smaller cell may be switched at higher speeds.

5.5.1. Collapsed Backbones

The next generation hub will provide an even more powerful integrated framework for managing enterprise internetworks. Although hubs will continue to provide the physical connectivity for workgroups and departments, a hub port will serve a single computer, and hub traffic will be concentrated to a single port on the internetworking switch (Figure 5.5). With collapsed backbones, problem isolation will be simplified because when failures occur, it will be obvious which computer failed. These sophisticated hubs will fundamentally change LAN design, connecting workstations directly to switches and providing a new level of visibility into network traffic. The switch will have router functionality because the higher-layer network management required will, typically, be in a centralized computer room (perhaps a basement). In Figure 5.5, Ethernet traffic previously used for interworkgroup or interdepartmental traffic is 'collapsed' onto the backplane of a centrally-located internetworking switch. Fiber runs vertically up on risers into a hub on each floor of the building. The hubs use Ethernet and token ring LANs employing unshielded-twisted pair wiring for access to each terminal. The fiber backbone supports the heavy traffic as well as injecting fault tolerance into the building internetwork.

5.6.   ENTERPRISE SWITCH

Intelligent hubs may soon be challenged by more powerful enterprise switches. Like a LAN hub, the switch segments LANs into more manageable parts. Commercially available switches now support between four and 90 ports with data rates from 45 to 155 Mb/s. Initially, the more powerful switches will have traditional asynchronous WAN inter-

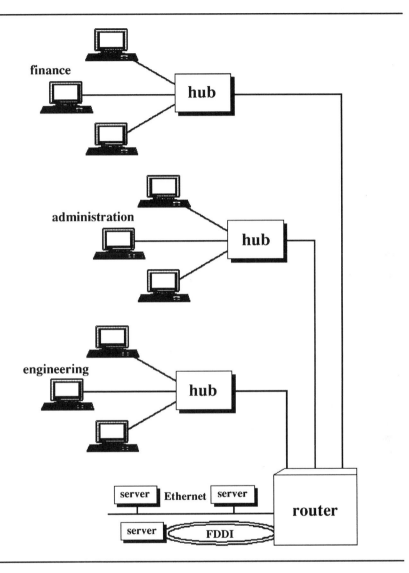

Figure 5.5.   Collapsed Backbone Network.

faces and support existing as well as more advanced network connections (Figure 5.6). Later, as newer switching fabrics such as ATM spread
throughout WANs and LANs, most interfaces will use ATM. The massively parallel architecture of an ATM switch allows concurrent switching along many parallel paths, giving each port full use of the allocated

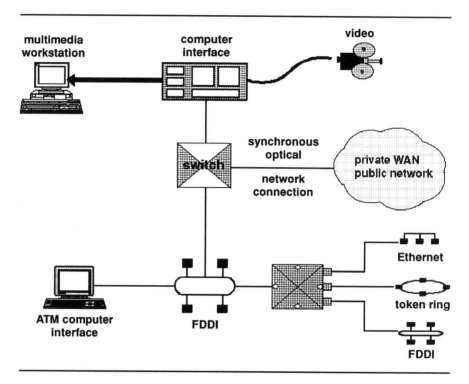

Figure 5.6. Enterprise switch network.

bandwidth. Employing cell switching, these switches break up data streams into very small units that are independently routed through the switch. This is done with hardware. The combination of cell switching and scaleable switching fabrics are key ingredients. Another is network management. Spanning the boundaries between LANs and WANs, the enterprise switch will offer sophisticated management, reducing the problems of changes and moves. Workgroup users can be registered together, regardless of their physical location. The switch automatically reconfigures the list of addresses when a registered network user plugs into a port, even when the new port is on a different LAN.

5.7. CONCLUSION

Although repeaters, gateways, routers, and bridges have evolved separately, they are coalescing into the LAN hub—which has the additional function of switching. The hub, in turn, will be eclipsed by the enterprise switch. On the basis of concurrent rather than shared media technology, such switches allocate full bandwidth to the user for the required interval. The importance of the enterprise switch will increase as more terminals are connected to hosts by means of LANs, more PCs are networked through LANs, and minicomputers, workstations, and mainframes are designed to use LANs as the primary host-to-host and host-to-front-end access method. All of these data sources have brought new traffic burdens to the WANs to which they connect.

This has led to a new hierarchy in WANs that allows the LAN to extend beyond its traditional boundaries. An extended LAN, the range of which may encompass a city or a metropolis, is referred to as a *metropolitan area network* (MAN). There is still considerable work required to flesh out the standards, particularly in the area of management. As first-generation LANs are phased out (over the rest of this decade), management problems will be resolved. Fiber LANs should become the preferred LAN for high-capacity private networks. SONET will facilitate interconnection of far-flung MANs. MAN traffic at the T 1, T 2, and T 3 rates will be able to access the SONET backbone via virtual tributaries, while data traffic at the FDDI rate of 100 Mb/s will be mapped onto a SONET/SDH OC-3 payload for transport to a remote MAN. At the same time, the WAN will rely less on circuit switching, as embodied in TDM-based multiplexers, and more on high-speed packet technologies. Before these new networks are detailed, the broadband technologies that make them possible will be described in Chapter 6.

6

Broadband Technologies

6.1. INTRODUCTION

Every application has an optimum-size data packet for transportation over a network. Real-time applications favor smaller packets, since smaller packet sizes are less likely to create bottlenecks. Most existing data networks favor larger packets to move larger chunks of data. With the X.25 slow-packet standard, some public carriers settled upon a 128-byte packet, because this gave the best network throughput when errors and retransmissions were considered. New packet transmission technologies are being deployed that achieve orders of magnitude greater than throughput rates of X.25. One such technology, fast-packet, is already a success in private T1 networks. Fast-packet is a generic term that is applied to many different high-speed transmission technologies (Figure 6.1). Fast-packet achieves high performance by eliminating many of the overhead functions carried out at intervening nodes by X.25. These networks exhibit low latency and very high-speed switching and thus are suitable for broadband communications. Frame relay is a fast-packet standard capable of transporting both small and large size packets at speeds up to T3.

6.1.1. Frame Relay

Frame relay operates at OSI model layers 1 and 2 and resembles LAN networking protocols. It assumes the customer is using error-correcting

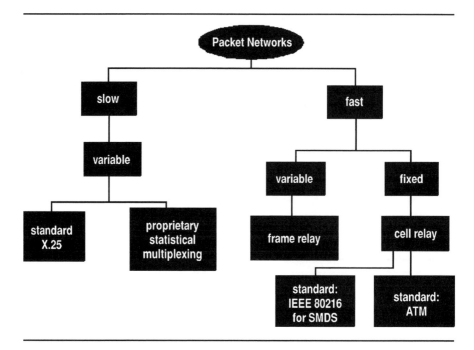

Figure 6.1.   Types of packet networks.

protocol suites such as the TCP/IP, IBM's SNA, Digital's DECnet, and Novell's IPX/SPX, among others, as well as relatively noiseless fiber and digital transmission. In contrast, X.25, developed for older analog leased lines, operates at OSI layers 1 through 3 and provides extensive error control. While it resembles a stripped down X.25, frame relay combines reduced overhead with high-speed interconnecting trunks, operating at DS0 rates and above. Overhead is reduced by eliminating the error checking and correction done in the data link (layer 2 of the OSI reference model) and moving the function of network layer 3 to increasingly intelligent end-stations (Figure 6.2). X.25 networks do extensive error checking and correction because they were designed to compensate for poor quality analog communication lines and dumb end-stations. For a packet network to work in that climate, it had to verify the integrity of the information it was transporting.

Among the differences in packet technologies, a primary one is the way in which the address and control field bits are used (Figure 6.3). By extending its address field, frame relay performs basic frame routing

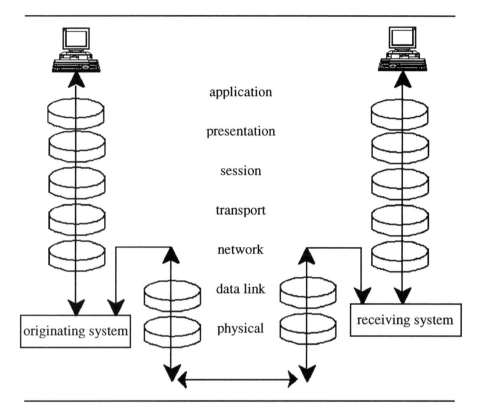

Figure 6.2.   OSI end-terminal interconnection.

and control within the data link layer. An abbreviated destination address is processed at each node by a frame handler that has a list of routes between end-stations. There are three key elements in the address field; the data link connection identifier (DLCI), the forward and backward explicit congestion notification (FECN/BECN) bits, and the discard eligibility bit (DE).

*   The DLCI that is instrumental in routing frames from one node to another identifies a frame's logical channel within a shared physical line. It defines a virtual circuit and its type—switched (SVC), permanent (PVC), or multicast (MVC). A DLCI terminates at the receiving port of a node and may be regenerated with a different value at the transmitting port as the frame travels node-to-node between two end-stations (Figure 6.4). Between nodes, a physical

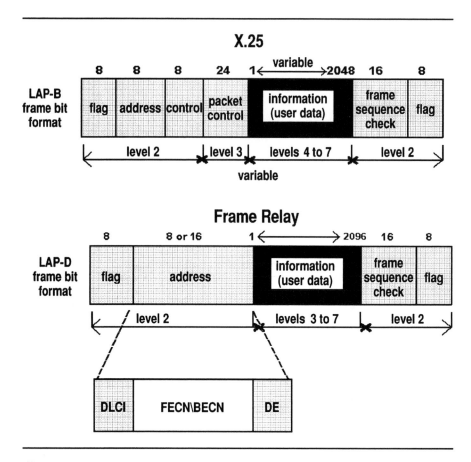

Figure 6.3.   WAN frame formats.

line can simultaneously support up to 1024 logical channels or connections. Depending on the network architecture, the number of
nodes, and the structure of the routing tables at each node, a frame
traveling from one end-station to another may use several DLCI
values before it reaches its destination.

• The BECN/FECN bits (and/or the DE bit) determine the network
response to congestion. When congestion occurs, a frame relay network may throttle traffic at the source, the destination, or both, to
control traffic flow. The BECN bit controls traffic at the source,
while the FECN bit initiates flow control at the destination.

• The DE bit sets the priority for frames to be discarded during peri-

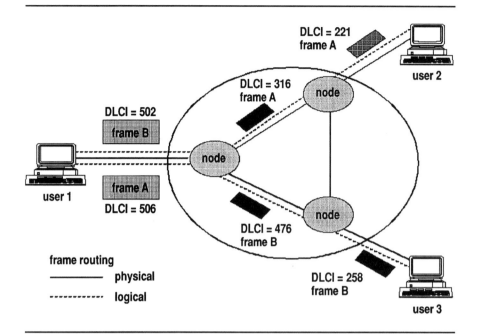

Figure 6.4.   Use of DLCI for transmission.

ods of congestion. Lower priority frames are discarded before higher priority frames.

6.1.2. Cell Relay

Cell relay employs tiny frames to transport information at even higher rates than frame relay. At the time of transmission, the cells are filled by data packets that arrive at irregular intervals (asynchronously). The line of cells itself is synchronous, transporting a continuous stream of data. But packets enter the stream only when they are available. The process resembles the loading of an endlessly circulating train of box cars. Each car in the train travels in sync with the others, but the rate at which information is loaded or removed is asynchronous. When there is a packet to ship, it drops into a car. At any one time, packets from different sources may contend for a specific box car, but only one packet can be loaded at a time. The rest must wait until a car is available, forming a *queue*. This process introduces a variable delay across the train. Sometimes there are many cars in a row, all filled with data packets. At other times only one car is filled, leaving a large gap between it and the next car containing a packet. Since an observer looking at the train in the middle of its run would not notice a reproducible pattern in the rate that the filled box cars pass, the cars or cells are deemed to be transferred asynchronously. The maximum rate that information travels is the rate at which the train is traveling.

When a user wants to send information to another user, that user signals the other with the cells. The first transmitted cell in the message contains the number of box cars of information. This cell goes to the destination. There it is removed and the destination sends a cell back to the source by a returning car. This cell defines the rate at which information may be transferred. For example, one box car full of information must be followed by five empty cars. This process, called *signaling*, is used to establish a connection and to negotiate throughput, grade of service, delays, and so on.

Cell relay uses small packets for high-speed, low-latency transport. Large amounts of information can be transmitted without monopolizing the network for long because the information is segmented. The cells are formed from much larger data words, rapidly switched and interleaved together. Software programming would be too slow for controlling this process, so the control vehicle is hardware. Silicon is the enabling technology. Cell segmentation and reassembly equipment would be too expensive without employing specialized silicon integrated circuits that are specifically designed for the task.

Several emerging broadband carrier services are based upon fixed- and variable-sized cells. Fixed-sized cells have several advantages over the variable-sized cells used in carrier services such as SMDS. Fixed-sized cells reduce the queuing delay for high-priority calls, since they are more rapidly processed at the user network interface. Fixed-sized cells are also switched more efficiently, which is the key to achieving the very high data rates achieved by the ATM form of cell relay.

6.2. ASYNCHRONOUS TRANSFER MODE (ATM)

Telcos/PTTs are migrating to standard network technologies to support the high bandwidth data communications needs of their business customers. Frame relay provides high-speed access, but lacks the capacity for a backbone Telco/PTT network. SONET/SDH networks have the bandwidth capacity, but lack the switching fabric. ATM fills this void. It was designed as a telecommunications technology, specifically as the transport for Broadband ISDN (BISDN). These standards define two ways to transfer blocks of information across a network—a synchronous transfer mode (STM) and an asynchronous transfer mode (ATM).

- STM, which should not be confused with SDH's STM-1, is a time division multiplexing method used in digital voice networks. It allocates time slots every 125 microseconds within a synchronously recurring frame. Multiplexing and switching equipment divide the total network bandwidth into a hierarchy of fixed-size channels such as DS0, DS1, DS2, DS3, etc. Each STM channel is identified by the position of its time slot(s) within the 125-microsecond frame.
- ATM allocates the total network bandwidth to services, flexibly sharing both bandwidth and time. ATM offers switching at a variety of speeds because it is not associated with a single media or transmission speed. Unlike STM, which breaks down bandwidth into channels of information, ATM transmits fixed-length packets of information or cells whenever a service requires bandwidth. It transports continuous bit-rate traffic such as voice and video as well as noncontinuous traffic such as the bursty data frequently encountered with LANs.

Despite the fact that it has been developed for public telephone networks, it is in LANs that ATM finds its first·application. As long as LAN users continue to transfer ever-larger data files and look to integrate isochronous voice traffic with data traffic, there is a great need for ATM. Nonetheless, its widespread use in LANs could still benefit the Telco/PTT. Carrying LAN traffic over WANs has been a challenge because LANs employ different technologies and have different transport needs than WANs. LANs rely on communication standards that support high data rates over relatively short distances. WANs use communications standards that work over longer distances, but are relatively slow. If WAN traffic becomes ATM-based and the same technology is used in the LAN, carriers will face a considerably easier task of integrating WAN and LAN traffic.

6.2.1. Broadband Switching

The ATM switching fabric is data-rate independent and supports both public network and LAN switching at ultra-high rates—exceeding 1 Gb/s. All ATM switching uses standard 53-byte cells. Each ATM cell has a five-byte header that contains virtual circuit and virtual path identifiers (Figure 6.5).

The header is transmitted first and contains the addressing infor-

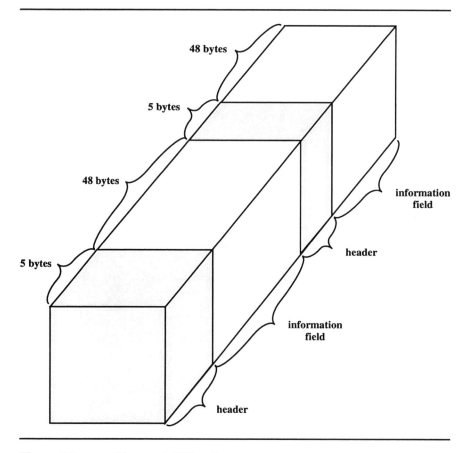

Figure 6.5.   Stream of ATM cells.

mation. It does not carry any service-specific data; rather, it defines the user/network interface by means of the following fields:

- Generic flow control (GFC)—the four-bit GFC is used for end-to-end flow control.
- Virtual channel identifier (VCI)—the VCI (16 bits) is similar to an X.25 virtual circuit; it defines a local logical connection between two ATM nodes.
- Virtual path identifier (VPI)—the VPI (eight bits) is an aggregate of VCIs.
- Payload type (PT)—the three-bit PT field indicates whether the cell payload contains user or network management information.

- Cell loss priority (CLP)—the one-bit CLP field indicates whether a cell can be discarded if the network becomes congested. If the CLP is set to one, the cell is subject to discard.
- Header error control (HEC)—the HEC uses an eight-bit error code to correct single-bit errors in the header, and to detect double-bit errors.

The information field (48 bytes) carries the payload within the cell.

6.2.2. ATM Standard Layers

The ATM standard defines three layers; the physical, ATM, and ATM adaptation layers (Figure 6.6).

6.2.2.1. Physical Layer. ATM cells may be transported over many different physical media and still maintain compatibility. The physical layer defines how ATM cell streams are transmitted over the physical media as well as the interface to the ATM layer. Cells are transported within the ATM layer either asynchronously, as in packet switching, or synchronously, as payloads encapsulated in SONET envelopes (Figure 6.7).

ATM Adaptation layer		- assembles and disassembles broadband services into a stream of cells
		- each cell has a header that contains routing information
ATM layer		- switches the cells around the network based on the routing information
Physical layer	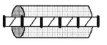	- provides the physical transportation of cells across the network

Figure 6.6.   ATM layers.

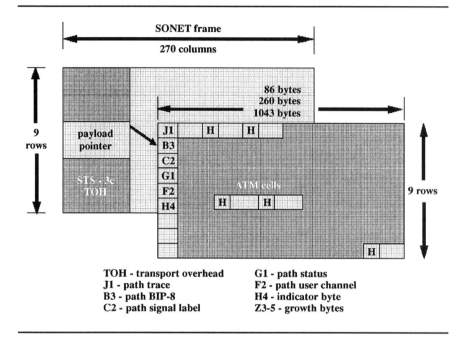

TOH - transport overhead   G1 - path status
J1 - path trace   F2 - path user channel
B3 - path BIP-8   H4 - indicator byte
C2 - path signal label   Z3-5 - growth bytes

Figure 6.7.   ATM Physical layer transport.

6.2.2.2. ATM Layer. The ATM layer provides the switching capability for the ATM cells by means of virtual connections. Two kinds of virtual connections have been standardized, virtual channel connections and virtual path connections. By reading the VPI and VCI bits in the header of each cell, an ATM switch routes cells to their destination. Virtual channels are grouped together to form a virtual path. Many virtual channels may share a single physical link at the same time. For example, all the virtual channels belonging to a customer may be bundled within a single virtual path, simplifying network management. A virtual channel may have other attributes associated with it, such as quality of service. Should congestion occur, the ATM switch selectively drops cells until the congestion clears.[5] The selection of which cells to lose is based on the guaranteed quality of service.

---

[5]Overload conditions may also be handled by a policing mechanism which limits services to their negotiated bandwidth.

6.2.2.3. ATM Adaptation Layer.   Above the cell switching layer are ATM adaptation layers (AAL), which map various kinds of traffic into and out of the cells. The adaptation layers are specialized to traffic types. A variable bit-rate adaptation layer handles data traffic; a constant bit rate adaptation layer handles voice and video traffic. The adaptation layers must differentiate between data, voice, and video traffic because of their very different transmission requirements. There are five types of AAL defined in the ATM Standard (Table 6.1). The AAL is still evolving. For example, AAL3/4 supports native BISDN. Later, AAL5 was constructed to support the use of BISDN for transport of existing protocol services at an even higher level of performance. AAL5 Services include:

• Notification of corrupted received AAL protocol data units (PDUs)
• Unverified data transfer (error recovery in higher layers)
• PDU transfer from one AAL to another

To provide a particular service, ATM maps the service into the information field of a cell. When the cell is full, the correct VCI/VPI information is placed in the header field and the cell enters the ATM cell stream. The AALs have two logical sublayers known as the *convergence sublayer* (CS) and the *segmentation and reassembly* sublayer (SAR) that support this process. The CS accepts data units from the ATM user interface and delivers the data units back after receiving it from the SAR. The SAR divides each data unit into cells on the segmentation side, and reconstructs incoming cells into data units on the reassembly side.

The CS ensures that the different types of traffic receive the right level of service at the user-to-network interface (UNI) and at the network-to-network interface (NNI). The CS passes PDUs on to the net-

Table 6.1.   ATM adaptation layer.

Feature	AAL1	AAL2	AAL3	AAL4	AAL5
Timing relation between source and destination	required	required	not required	not required	not required
Bit rate	constant	variable	variable	variable	variable
Connection mode	connect-oriented	connect-oriented	connect-oriented	connection-less	connect-oriented

user data	PAD	control field	length field	CRC-32
(up to 64K bytes)	(0 – 47 bytes)	(2 bytes)	(2 bytes)	(4 bytes)

Figure 6.8.   Protocol data unit structure.

work from the UNI and delivers PDUs back after reception (Figure 6.8). The SAR sublayer divides each PDU into cells during segmentation and reconstructs incoming cells into PDU during reassembly. When transmitting into the network, the CS appends a PDU trailer and pads the PDU plus trailer in multiples of 48 bytes. The trailer contains a cyclic redundancy check field (CRC-32), a PDU length field, and a control field. Cells formed during the AAL layer segmentation process will all be 48 bytes. The SAR reassembles incoming cells into complete PDUs before passing them to the CS. Information for the reassembly is obtained from a combination of the VPI/VCI fields and end-of-message indicator encoded in the PT field. After the CRC-32 is verified, the PDU is delivered to the ATM user.

6.3.   CONCLUSION

With hundreds of millions of desktop computers connected in millions of LANs worldwide, it was natural for the LANs to be connected, first in geographically close areas, later in metropolises, then in nations and around the world. It was not just LAN computer traffic that was infused into the WAN, but computer technology also. The LAN topologies, high bandwidths, stripped down protocols, open architectures, and management were adopted by the WAN. New broadband technologies such as frame and cell relay, SONET/SDH, and ATM entered the Telco/PTT networks. ATM, for example, allows the Telco/PTT to tailor a variety of services to the specific needs of business and residential customers. Now the same technologies, honed in the WAN, are returning to the LAN mainstream, routing information at unprecedented speeds.

7

Transmission

7.1. INTRODUCTION

The widespread use of digital technology in the WAN occurred because bandwidth was—and is—expensive. Encouraged by favorable tariffs, users have upgraded to digital services. Now this growth is accelerating because of the benefits offered by advanced digital data communications protocols. The protocols, first deployed in the computing environment, are being modified to create synchronous overlays to the global asynchronous telephone network.

The Telco/PTT use of asynchronous protocols derives from worldwide networking standards implemented over the past 40 years. These protocols operate at the physical level (OSI layer 1) and are transparent to the computer communication protocols they transport. In North America, for example, the standard for high-speed WAN interconnection is the T1, with a fixed bit rate of 1.544 Mb/s. This rate supports 24 digital channels of 64 kb/s each, plus eight kb/s for signaling. At the time of T1 service introduction, 64 kb/s was the bandwidth needed to transport a single voice conversation, using a method of modulation called *pulse code modulation* (PCM). Today, toll-quality voice can be compressed even further, allowing a 64 kb/s channel to carry multiple voice conversations. Nonetheless, the fundamental rate for voice transmission and switching in the public telephone network remains 64 kb/s.

Within the public telephone network there is a hierarchy of rates that go beyond T1, referred to as the *asynchronous standard hierarchy*.

While consistent at each level, it has little overlap, so asynchronous DS1 frames have little resemblance to DS3 frames.[6] As a result, the public network is synchronous only on a piecemeal basis, and therefore lacks the management capability and bandwidth flexibility for many newly demanded services. In contrast, LANs provide inexpensive connectivity, at least in a local area. But LANs, too, have come under pressure from the increasing bandwidth demands of new applications.

One result is a tenfold increase in bandwidth and use of fiber media. FDDI, a dual counter-rotating token ring topology LAN operating over fiber, is being promoted as a solution for broadband applications. But shared-media LANs of any variety are intrinsically limited. Video, as well as voice traffic, tolerates relatively small delays and requires synchronization signals that shared-media LANs lack. In campus networks, for example, video cannot be effectively transported, even with compression as low as 128 kb/s. If there are only a few workstations on an FDDI LAN, such compression might be enough, but that is not what happens in a shared-media environment.

7.2. BROADBAND ASYNCHRONOUS TRANSMISSION: T3/ E3

T3, an asynchronous transmission service, represents the equivalent of 28 T1 lines at a rate of 44.736 Mb/s. Although offered by Telcos/PTTs, there are issues to consider before deploying T3 in corporate networks: First, asynchronous signal types bear no relationship to each other. Within a 45 Mb/s DS3 signal, the 1.5 Mb/s DS1 signal has no visibility. The entire DS3 has to be taken apart to get at the DS1. Then the signal has to be reframed, taking time and processing power. Second, DS3 is often transmitted over fiber, which requires an interface for electrical-to-optical signal conversion. Unfortunately, asynchronous transmission only provides a standard electrical interface. The lack of an optical standard for asynchronous signals has led to many proprietary interfaces.[7] These proprietary optic transmission rates include 45 Mb/s (typically 48 to 50 Mb/s), 90 Mb/s, 135 Mb/s, 405 Mb/s, 560 Mb/s, 565 Mb/s, and 1.1 Gb/s—all of which are unique to individual terminal equipment

---

[6]T1 = one DS1; T2 = four DS1; T3 = 28 DS1.

[7]T3 services require the customer to negotiate with the carrier regarding the type of optical interfaces to be placed in the interexchange carrier's serving office.

vendors. The T3 rate of 44.736 Mb/s represents the North American standard. The Japanese T3 equivalent is 32 Mb/s, while the European equivalent is E3, which operates at 34 Mb/s and supports E1 signals at 2.048 Mb/s transmission rates. Both E3 and T3 run out of steam when intelligent networks are considered. Although there is some capability for maintenance signaling, T3/E3 actually have less maintenance visibility than lower-rate T1/E1.

The situation is changing for the better. Rather than jury-rigging the asynchronous standards for improved management capability, a more general approach was taken by the worldwide standards bodies. Networks have begun the migration from asynchronous to synchronous transmission. With the almost inexhaustible bandwidth of fiber, the silicon revolution, and the improved synchrony of network clocks, both packet-switched and isochronous traffic can be transported synchronously over large distances. Today, a variety of networking technologies is available to address the rapidly emerging class of *bandwidth-ravenous applications*. These broadband networking technologies include the fast-packet schemes, such as frame and cell relay (ATM) previously discussed, and SONET/SDH. SONET/SDH represent a transmission format that includes in-band network management, and overlays the existing asynchronous broadband network, and will eventually replace it.

7.3. SONET AND SDH

The asynchronous standards specify the termination and aspects of a limited amount of network management. Access to the network is specified as a standard electrical interface for connection compatibility. For DS3, the rate of 44.736 Mb/s is defined, together with a signal level, impedance, and so forth. This is not adequate to achieve interoperability among equipment vendors (Figure 7.1). Both SONET and SDH standards specify the electrical and optical interfaces as well as protocols at different points on the communication line, permitting the use of equipment from different vendors anywhere along the fiber span (Figure 7.2). This capability is referred to as *mid-span meet*. Customers get better bandwidth control *and* Telco/PTT reduced costs because SONET/SDH–compliant equipment is interoperable. Moreover, its ability to concatenate signals consistently at any speed makes multiplexing sufficiently low-cost to be embedded in fiber optic equipment. Given this, real-time switchable multiplexers, add/drop systems, and ring networks can now be built for improved network reliability, performance, and cost. As a result, SONET (in North America) and SDH (in Europe)

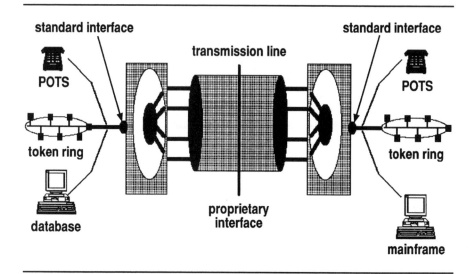

Figure 7.1. Asynchronous connection.

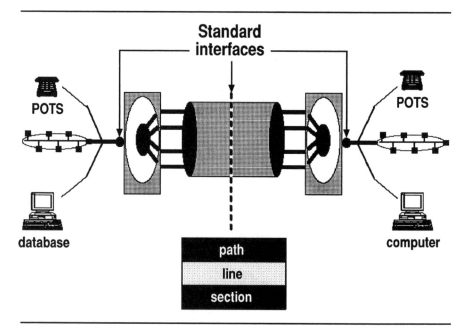

Figure 7.2. Synchronous connection by SONET.

deployment is gaining great momentum and could reach parity with the asynchronous market by 1997, equating to many billions of dollars.

7.3.1. Network Architecture

SONET/SDH technology combines the historical elements of LANs and WANs. Much is borrowed from advanced computer technology. For example, the SONET in-band network management ASN.1 protocol derives from the OSI standards on object language definition that was developed for computers. This characterization by a communications standards body reflects the coalescing of LAN and WAN technology. Due to its powerful architecture, SONET integrates existing point-to-point fiber links into true networks, enabling them to route single-voice grade channels digital service level Ø (DS0) without the need for multiple stages of multiplexing and demultiplexing. The eventual role of SONET and fiber systems is not simply to replace the dedicated copper lines used in transmitting multiplexed digital signals; SONET networks will simultaneously provide greater functionality, standardized fiber interfaces, higher transmission speeds and reduced maintenance. SONET provides a flexible, controllable network with centralized network management. Because of its capacity to manage large amounts of bandwidth, as well as its simplicity and cost-effectiveness, SONET will eventually freeze purchases of non standard fiber and asynchronous communications equipment. It already is the preferred delivery vehicle for a number of emerging broadband services, including frame relay, SMDS, BISDN, and ATM (Figure 7.3).

For this vision of broadband networking to be fully realized, the Telcos/PTTs will have to upgrade their infrastructure to support SONET signals that operate at higher data rates than their asynchronous counterparts. This will require the gradual replacement of the asynchronous network infrastructure: although the asynchronous network is unable to support SONET signals, SONET will transport the asynchronous signals such as DS1, DS1C, DS2, and DS3. Therefore, existing asynchronous gear will not have to be replaced as SONET equipment migrates into the public network. And the ongoing deployment of SONET equipment will lower the cost of bandwidth, recouping the Telco/PTT investment.

7.3.2. Transmission Rates

Using a basic building block called the *synchronous transport signal level-1* (STS-1), with a line rate of 51.840 Mb/s for SONET and 155.52 Mb/s for synchronous transport mode level-1 (STM-1) for SDH, SONET/

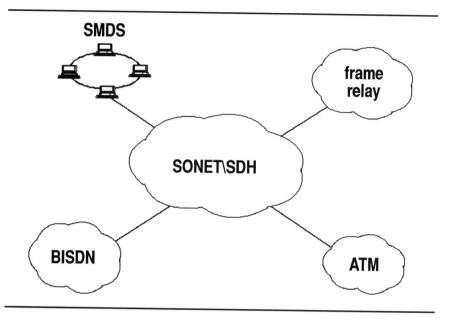

Figure 7.3.   SONET transport for emerging services.

SDH reaches 2.488 gigabits per second in exact multiples of STS-1. Table 7.1 shows the relationship of line rates, payload, overhead bandwidths, and the corresponding STS levels.[8] STS electrical signals, when transmitted over fiber, are converted to a corresponding optical signal called optical carrier (OC). For example, higher SONET transmission rates are established by concatenating "N" STS-1s to form an STS-N. Currently, "N" is defined as one, three, 12, 24, 36 and 48, but rates up to OC-255 or 13.2192 Gb/s are possible.

7.3.3. Synchronous Clocks

Unlike asynchronous signals, the synchronous signal is not demultiplexed and then remultiplexed at every central office through which it passes. SONET allows simple add/drop multiplexing. That is, information as fine as a single DS0 can be taken from one broadband data stream and inserted in another. This process requires clock synchrony within the public tele-

---

[8]SONET, a North American ANSI and Japan Standard, uses STS signal hierarchy. The European CCITT equivalent, SDH, uses the STM signal hierarchy.

Table 7.1.   **SONET rates and bandwidths.**

OC	STS	Rates (Mb/s)		
Optical	Electrical	Line	Payload	Overhead
OC–1	STS–1	51.840	50.122	1.728
OC–3	STS–3	155.520	150.336	5.184
OC–9	STS–9	466.560	451.008	15.552
OC–12	STS–12	622.080	601.344	20.736
OC–18	STS–18	933.120	902.016	31.104
OC–24	STS–24	1244.160	1202.688	41.472
OC–36	STS–36	1866.240	1804.032	62.208
OC–48	STS–48	2488.320	2405.376	82.944
OC–96	STS–96	4976.640	4810.752	165.888
OC–192	STS–192	9953.280	9621.504	331.776

phone network. SONET equipment receives timing from Stratum 3 or better-quality clocks (Table 7.2). When the asynchronous public network was designed, such clocks did not exist—delays in then–available vacuum tubes and transistors were too great. Fortunately, it is possible today for accurate clocks to be distributed across thousands of kilometers, making synchronous transmission feasible.

7.4.   LAYERED STRUCTURE

The overhead is divided into three layers—path, line, and section—that govern the transport of the payload across the network (Figure 7.4). The relationship between SONET layers plays a very important role

Table 7.2.   **Public telephone network clock hierarchy.**

Stratum	Accuracy	Network Element
1	.01 part in one billion	Cesium clock
2	16 parts in one billion	electronic switching systems (ESS)
3	4.6 parts in one billion	digital cross-connect system (DCS)
4	32 parts in one billion	digital private branch exchange (DPBX)

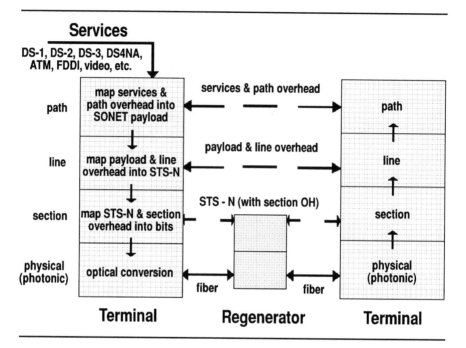

Figure 7.4.   Layered networks.

with regard to the various network services, DS-1, DS-3, etc., that are supported.

7.4.1. Physical Layer

The physical layer transports bits as optical pulses through the fiber medium. No overhead is associated with this layer. The main function of the physical layer is to receive the STS-N signal bit stream, convert each bit into an optical pulse, and transmit the optical pulse across the fiber medium towards the far-end terminal. Key concerns are pulse shape, power levels, and the line code for error detection and recovery.

7.4.2. Section Layer

The section layer transports the STS-N frame across the physical medium. It uses the physical layer for transport. Section layer functions include framing, scrambling, section overhead processing, and error monitoring. The overhead defined for this layer is interpreted or created by section terminating equipment (STE).

7.4.3. Line Layer

The line layer is responsible for transporting the payload and the line overhead to its peer at the far end. All lower layers provide transport. This layer maps the payload and the line overhead into STS-N frames. The payloads and line overheads are synchronized and multiplexed within the STS-N, before the STS-N signal is passed to the section layer. The overhead associated with this layer is interpreted or created by line terminating equipment (LTE).

7.4.4. Path Layer

Transport of network services between two SONET multiplexing nodes is the function of the path layer. Examples of such services are the provisioning of DS1, DS2, DS3, DS-4NA, FDDI, ATM, video, etc. The path layer maps the services into the SONET payload format as required by the line layer, and communicates end-to-end via the path overhead. The path terminating equipment (PTE) interprets or creates the overhead defined for this layer.

7.5.   SECTION, LINE, PATH STRUCTURE

Section, line and path are structures that delineate portions of the fiber optic transmission facility. These interconnect the SONET network elements (Figure 7.5).

7.5.1. Section

Section is the segment of SONET transmission facility that includes terminating points between a network element and a regenerator, or two regenerators.

7.5.2. Line

Line, with LTE, transports information between two consecutive line terminating network elements; one that originates, and another that terminates the line signal. For example, in Figure 7.5 this represents the sections between the add/drop multiplexer (ADM) or digital cross-connect (DCS) and the terminal multiplexer (TM).

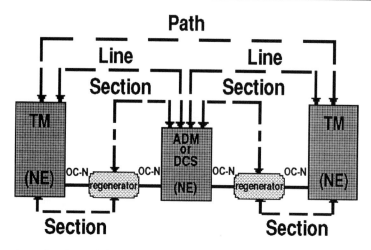

TM = terminal multiplexer   ADM = add/drop mutiplexer

DCS = digital cross-connect   NE = network element

Figure 7.5.   Section, line, and path.

7.5.3. Path

The path is defined as a logical connection between two points; one (source) at which the frame is assembled, and another where it is disassembled (sink). For example, the link between the two TM's in Figure 7.5 is called a *path*. The SONET/SDH path and line section manages heterogeneous environments, providing end-to-end control by means of the frame overhead bytes. The actual overhead byte values depend upon how the equipment will be used. For instance, the K1 and K2 bytes transport messages between the network elements and the network management system. With a ring topology, a more sophisticated K1/K2 protocol would be required to switch traffic direction, since the traditional alarming protocol of the telephone network would be incompatible with a ring architecture.[9]

---

[9]This topology was previously limited to LANs because alarm protocols of the public telephone network such as *far-end receive* did not apply.

7.6.   SONET FRAMES

The lowest data rate supported by SONET/SDH is the 51.840 Mb/s STS-1 frame. An STS-1 frame is a nine-row by 90-column byte matrix structure totaling 810 bytes, or 6480 bits (Figure 7.6). The byte from row one, column one is transmitted first, then is followed by row one, column two, and so on. The transmission is from left column to right column and from top row to bottom row. The STS-1 frame transmission duration is 125 microseconds, or 8000 frames per second, which maintains compatibility with the existing telephone network. The first three columns, or 27 bytes, are assigned to the transport overhead, which is further subdivided into section overhead (nine bytes) and line overhead (18 bytes). The remaining nine rows by 87 columns constitute the STS-1 synchronous payload envelope (SPE) that has a total of 783 bytes. Of

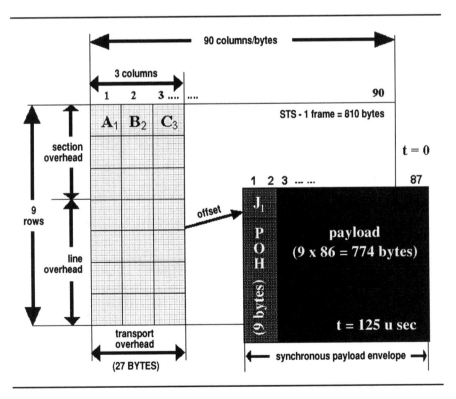

Figure 7.6.   STS-1 format.

these, nine bytes in the first column are designated as STS path over-head, or POH. The actual payload is 774 bytes, which results in a total of 49.536 Mb/s of payload capacity.

This payload capacity is used to carry a DS3 signal at 44.736 Mb/s, or 28 DS1s each, at 1.544 Mb/s. All this is at STS-1 level. For transport of payloads with bandwidth requirements greater than STS-1, several STS-1s can be combined or concatenated (byte interleaved) and trans-ported as a single entity. For example, the CCITT has defined the SDH lowest-rate STM-1 as the equivalent to SONET STS-3.

Before byte interleaving, the STS-1s are frame-aligned so the trans-port overhead of each STS-1 can be combined to form an STS-N transport overhead. Thus, all transport overheads are frame-aligned, while the individual payloads float within the envelope as indicated by the respec-tive payload pointers within each STS-1 transport overhead. The byte interleaved STS-N signal, when transmitted, results in an optical signal called Optical Carrier OC-N, with values of N. The overhead byte C1 in the section overhead identifies the STS-1 within an STS-N frame format.

The transport overhead (TOH), together with section and line overheads, performs the functions needed to transport the synchronous payload envelope (SPE) over the fiber link. Also, the payload pointer, or *offset*, resides within the line overhead of the TOH. The payload pointer plays a very crucial role in the transmission process because it indicates the start of the STS-1 SPE. It also permits the payload to float within the envelope, and helps adjust frequency deviations between network elements. A nine-byte path overhead (POH) is allocated within the syn-chronous payload envelope to support transport of the payload from the point at which it is assembled to the point at which it is disassembled.

The size of an STS-N frame is N times the STS-1 frame size or N × 810 bytes (Figure 7.7). Similarly,

- transport overhead = $N \times 27$ bytes
- synchronous payload envelope = $N \times 783$ bytes
- path overhead = $N \times 9$ bytes
- Payload size = $N \times 774$ bytes

7.6.1. STS-Nc Concatenation Format

The structure for STS-Nc concatenation is illustrated in Figure 7.8. SONET accommodates higher transmission rates by synchronously byte interleav-ing 'N' STS-1s to form an STS-N signal. Each STS-1 within the STS-N, however, remains a separate entity that is assembled at the source and

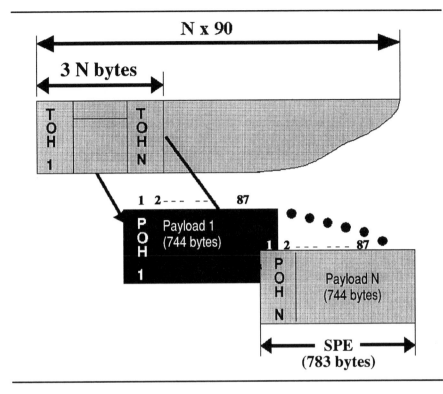

Figure 7.7.   STS-N frame format.

disassembled at the sink point. The size of an STS-Nc is $N \times 810$ bytes, while the transport overhead is $N \times 27$ bytes. Both overhead and payload are treated as single entities. Only one path overhead (POH) is shown. The remainder is allocated to the payload that, in this case, is $(N \times 783 - 9)$ bytes. Further, in the STS-Nc frame format, the first STS-1 carries a normal pointer in its transport overhead, while the pointers of other STS-1s, forming the STS-Nc, carry the concatenation indicator. This indicator helps in binding the constituent STS-1s together and multiplexing, switching, and transporting them as a single entity. A concatenation indicator in the transport overhead shows that the STS-1s of an STS-Nc are joined—and will remain—together until terminated. By byte interleaving 'N' STS-1s, SONET provides for super rate services, such as BISDN, which uses multiples of the STS-1 rate.

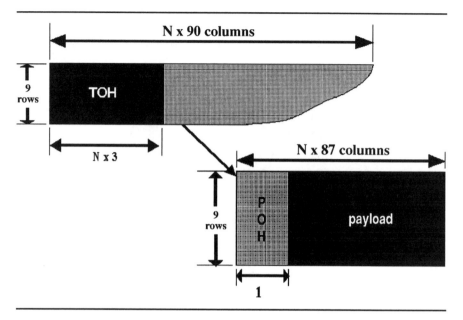

Figure 7.8.   STS-Nc concatenation format.

7.6.2.   Section, Line, and Path Overheads

In the STS-1 frame format, the transport overhead (TOH) consists of 27 bytes, of which nine are assigned to section overhead and 18 to line overhead. These bytes occupy the first three columns of the STS-1 frame. The POH has nine bytes. These form the first column of the synchronous payload envelope (SPE). The section overhead is created or modified within the section segment, the line overhead within the line segment, and the path overhead within the path segment. Each layer, section, line, or path processes the associated overhead prior to being inserted in the signal. Each overhead assists the transport of the STS-N signal between two end points of the transmission segment. Figure 7.9 shows the details of section, line and path overheads.

7.6.2.1.   Section Overhead.

- A1 and A2 bytes provide STS-1 framing synchronization.
- C1 byte identifies each STS-1 within an STS-N.
- B1 byte is used for section error monitoring.

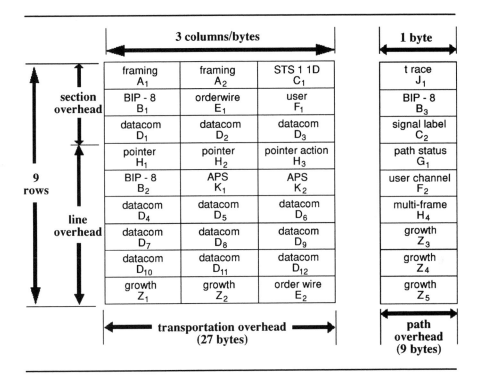

3 columns/bytes			1 byte
framing A_1	framing A_2	STS 1 1D C_1	t race J_1
BIP - 8 B_1	orderwire E_1	user F_1	BIP - 8 B_3
datacom D_1	datacom D_2	datacom D_3	signal label C_2
pointer H_1	pointer H_2	pointer action H_3	path status G_1
BIP - 8 B_2	APS K_1	APS K_2	user channel F_2
datacom D_4	datacom D_5	datacom D_6	multi-frame H_4
datacom D_7	datacom D_8	datacom D_9	growth Z_3
datacom D_{10}	datacom D_{11}	datacom D_{12}	growth Z_4
growth Z_1	growth Z_2	order wire E_2	growth Z_5

section overhead · line overhead · 9 rows

◄── transportation overhead ──►
(27 bytes)

path overhead
(9 bytes)

Figure 7.9.   Section, line, and path overheads.

- E1 provides a local channel for voice communications.
- F1 byte is reserved for the network provider.
- D1, D2, and D3 bytes provide a 192 kb/s data communications channel (DCC) for section operation, administration, maintenance, and provisioning.

7.6.2.2. Line Overhead.

- H1 and H2 bytes are used as pointers to the start of the STS-1 synchronous payload envelope (SPE).
- H3 byte provides for SPE frequency adjustment in conjunction with H1 and H2 bytes.
- B2 is used for line error monitoring.
- K1 & K2 bytes provide automatic protection switching.
- D4 to D12 bytes form the 576 kb/s data communications channel for line operations, administration, maintenance, and provisioning.

- Z1 & Z2 bytes are reserved for future growth.
- E2 provides an express orderwire channel between line entities.

7.6.2.3. Path Overhead.

- J1 byte is used to verify connection continuity between the receiver/transmitter pair.
- B3 is used for path error monitoring.
- C2 indicates the 'equipped/unequipped' status of STS-1.
- G1 byte is used to monitor status and performance of the end-to-end path.
- F2 is reserved for the network provider.
- H4 byte indicates phases within the STS-1 frame.
- Z3, Z4, and Z5 bytes are reserved for future growth.

This overhead structure provides a powerful fault-detection, sectionalization, and reconfiguration capability. The embedded operations channel (EOC) within the data communications channel (DCC) allows remote control of the operations, administration, maintenance, and provisioning functions for interconnected SONET network elements, reducing the need to dispatch technicians. The embedded operations channel (EOC) protocol follows the seven-layer model for OSI and thus permits interworking with intelligent OSI network controllers.

7.6.3. Virtual Tributaries

SONET framing accommodates lower-rate signals, providing transport for existing North American and international formats. The STS-1 payload may be subdivided into smaller Virtual Tributaries (VTs) that transport signals at less than DS3. Each VT functions as a separate container within the STS-1 signal with its own overhead bits. Because SONET/SDH is an international standard, the most common North American (DS-1 at 1.544 Mb/s) and international (E-1 at 2.048 Mb/s) tributaries have defined VT mappings. Less common tributaries, such as DS1C and DS-2, are also represented. There is a special mapping for higher-rate DS3 signals within a SONET payload—and eventually 10 Mb/s for Ethernet and 16 Mb/s for token ring LANs.

There are both 'locked' and 'floating'—as well as channelized and unchannelized—VT modes. The unchannelized floating mode is for wideband cross-connection down to the DS1 level. In unchannelized operation, the lowest addressable level is a VT. Two unchannelized mappings have been defined: asynchronous and bit synchronous. The former requires minimum timing consistency between the tributaries and the SONET clock, whereas the latter establishes a common clock frequency, but assigns an arbitrary phase. The locked mode fixes the VT location within the SPE that supports DS1 cross-connects. DS0 channels are uniquely addressable within a SONET payload by means of channelization. This is also known as *byte-synchronous* operation, in which both a fixed clock frequency and a fixed phase are established, based upon the DS1 frame. This enables individual DS0s (eight-bit bytes) to be easily identified and cross-connected. The channelized locked mode provides for DS0 level cross-connection and bridging into an existing DS3 network. The floating mode employs pointers that define the location of the VT. An advantage of VT pointers is that they remove the need for slip buffers. In SONET equipment, the synchronizer, desynchronizer, and slip buffer are replaced by a pointer processor.

A VT group architecture accommodates the mixes of various VT types within an SPE. The VT group size is constant at nine rows by 12 columns, or 108 bytes. Mixing VT types within the same group is not allowed, but the number of VTs within a VT group depends on the VT size. For example, four VT-1.5s, three VT-2s, two VT-3s, or one VT-6 may be packaged into a single VT group, and seven VT groups may be byte interleaved with the overhead to form the SPE.

7.6.4. SONET Standards

Lightwave fiber optic digital transport systems have been used for decades. Nonstandard or proprietary transmission rates of 90, 140, 405, 565, and 810 Mb/s, and 1.2 and 1.7 Gb/s, are deployed within these optical communications networks. The Exchange Carriers Standards Association's (ECSA) T1 committee was established in 1984 to coordinate the development of U.S. telecommunications standards. American National Standards Institute (ANSI) fully supports this ECSA/T1 committee, and further, the SONET specifications comply with the Consultative Committee on International Telephony and Telegraphy's (CCITT) Synchronous Digital Hierarchy (SDH) recommendations. CCITT is the United Nations body that makes recommendations and coordinates the development of telecommunications standards for the entire world. Although there are differences between the two standards, particularly in the areas of rates and management, they are mostly compatible.

SONET is the North American standard and SDH is the international standard. Both are being cooperatively developed. The standards are being released in phases due to their complexity, worldwide scope, and collaborative nature. Due to this phased SONET/SDH standardization, vendors are designing equipment that can be readily upgraded to conform to emerging standards. The Phase I Standard was released in 1988 by the T1 committee.

7.6.4.1. Phase I.   Phase I has two components—T1.105 and T1.106.

T1.105 defines:

- byte interleaved multiplexing format
- line rates for STS—1, 3, 9, 12, 18, 24, 36, and 48
- mappings for DS0, DS1, DS2, DS3
- monitoring mechanisms for section, line and path structures
- 192 kb/s and 576 kb/s data communications channels (DCC)

In addition, T1.106 specifies the optical parameters for the long-reach single mode fiber cable systems.

7.6.4.2. Phase II.   Phase II standards, released during 1990/1991, have three components, namely—T1.105R1, T1.117, and T1.102-199X.

T1.105R1 is a revision of the earlier T1.105 and specifies:

- SONET format clarification and enhancements
- timing and synchronization enhancements
- automatic protection switching (APS)
- seven-layer protocol stack for DCC and embedded operations channels
- mapping of DS-4 (139 Mb/s) signal into STS-3c

In addition, T1.117 specifies the optical parameters for short-haul (less than two kilometers) multimode, fiber cable systems, and T1.102-199X gives electrical specifications for STS-1 and STS-3 signals.

The Phase I and II specifications have sufficient detail to initiate development of SONET integrated circuit chip sets by several new device vendors. The vendors are using several silicon technologies to cope with the wide spread in bit rates. At the low end (up to 622 Mb/s, or OC-12), CMOS, BiCMOS and ECL gate arrays satisfy the performance requirements. Gigabit-per-second speeds require high-powered sub-micron bipolar and Gallium- Arsenide (GaAs) technology, which is more costly. Because of integrated circuits, network elements such as add/drop multiplexers (ADM), digital cross-connects (DCS), and remote digital terminals (RDT), among others, are commercially available.

7.6.4.3. Phase III.   Phase III addresses synchronization; network survivability; service mapping; operations, administration, maintenance, and provisioning message sets; and DCC/LAN standardization and ad-

dressing (Figure 7.10). Perhaps most crucial and controversial is the issue of communication over the embedded operations channel. Without this standard, equipment from different vendors cannot exchange control information. This was evident in the first demonstration of a midspan meet between two SONET fiber systems using diverse vendor equipment (Alcatel & Fujitsu) in the Contel Technology Center, December 1990. Traffic was successfully passed at the OC-1 and OC-3 rates, but network management commands could not be exchanged. SONET interfaces are incredibly intelligent. The NEs gather information about their own condition, the performance of signals that pass through them, and assign bandwidth flexibly. A single NE can contain over 20,000 separate registers to store this information. All is wasted if there is no way of getting the information out of the NE into an operations support

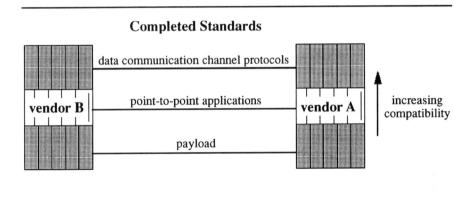

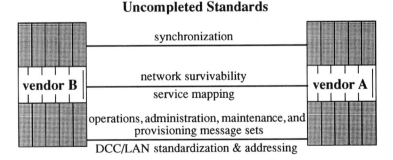

Figure 7.10.   SONET standardization.

system (OSS) that can interpret the data and take appropriate action. The SONET interface provides a standardized communications channel at 172 kb/s in the section layer and 576 kb/s in the line layer for this purpose. Every network element processes the section data communications channel (DCC), and the line terminating network elements, such as multiplexers, can process the line DCC.

Without resolution of the operations, administration, maintenance, and provisioning message format, existing Regional Bell operating companies (RBOC) operational support systems cannot work with SONET network management. The SONET OSS is still being defined for operations, administration, maintenance and provisioning of network services. For a NE to communicate with an OSS, two basic functions are required. First, there must be agreement on the protocols used to reliably transfer information from the network element to the OSS. For SONET, a full seven-layer protocol stand has been standardized and is contained in ANSI T1.105-1991. Protocols used in each of the seven layers are recognized standards. Second is the format for the messages used to inform the OSS of NE conditions. Present RBOC OSS's use the ASCII-based Transaction Language 1 (TL1) which is a man-to-machine language. SONET network applications require a machine-to-machine language, such as CMISE/ASN.1, organized around data structures. Resolution of this OSS issue is crucial for the completion of the SONET standards.

Phase III is not fully defined, but will likely consist of three components; T1.xxx, T1.106R1, and T1.105R2.

- T1.xxx will define the SONET operations, administration, maintenance, and provisioning messages that pass over the EOC. Progress is being made toward a generic network model required for OSS and NE communications, as well as the architecture, protocol procedures, and functional requirements for an operations, administration, maintenance, and provisioning management system. (In addition to management methods, the transport of LAN frames, such as the mapping of a 125 Mb/s FDDI signal into a 155 Mb/s STS-3c SONET signal, is a Phase III issue.)
- T1.106R1 will be a revision of T1.106, issued earlier for the purpose of more closely aligning SONET with CCITT SDH recommendations.
- The following issues are targeted to be specified under T1.105R2, a revision of T1.105R1: nested automatic protection switching (APS); ring APS; STS-N tandem path capability; VTx concatenation; and 622 Mb/s ATM (BISDN and 802.6).

7.7.   CONCLUSION

The Synchronous Optical Network (SONET) embodiment was conceived at Bellcore in 1984. SONET standards remain in development and are arriving in three phases. Phase I standards, issued in 1988, have permitted the development and testing of early SONET equipment. Phase II standards are being formalized now. Phase III, the final step, is expected to be approved in 1994 or later. Major issues to be resolved include ways for disparate vendor equipment to exchange network management information and be monitored by operations support systems (OSS).

Due to its powerful architecture, SONET will integrate existing point-to-point fiber links into true networks that will route single voice-grade channels (DS0) through the network without the need for multiple stages of multiplexing and demultiplexing. The eventual role of SONET and fiber systems is not simply to replace dedicated copper

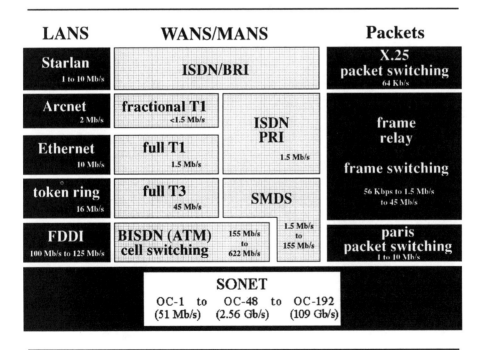

Figure 7.11.   SONET service infrastructure.

lines used in transmitting multiplexed digital signals (DS1, DS3, etc.) between two points, but simultaneously to provide greater functionality, standardized fiber interfaces, higher transmission speeds, and reduced operational labor requirements. With SONET, fiber, for the first time, will fully take its place as part of the international telecommunications network fabric. Only then will we have a flexible, controllable network with centralized network management, supporting features such as *bandwidth on demand.*

Because of its capacity to manage large amounts of bandwidth, combined with simplicity and cost-effectiveness, SONET will, in a few years, totally displace the existing installed base of nonstandard fiber and electronic equipment. Since SONET is a transport technology, it does not necessarily displace emerging technologies such as frame relay, SMDS, FDDI, BISDN and ATM, which can and will be carried by the SONET network (Figure 7.11).

8

SONET Elements & Networks

8.1. INTRODUCTION

SONET networks will embrace a mix of equipment from different suppliers, span the interconnect or midspan meet between different carriers, and bridge public and private networks. Features like direct multiplexing and grooming of DS0s, add/drop capabilities, and standard optical interfaces will simplify the design and management of broadband networks. SONET equipment will form the tributaries, interoffice trunks, metropolitan and suburban backbones of public and private broadband networks. The topologies include:

- Point-to-point networks that concentrate traffic from tributaries.
- Drop/insert networks that use simplified multiplexing to eliminate the need for back-to-back multiplexers.
- Ring networks with drop and insert capability so that traffic can be sent to a central office, backhauled, and quickly restored in case of failures.
- Star networks with a central hub and branches extending to remote locations.
- Hybrid networks that use a combination of the above topologies.

8.2. SONET MULTIPLEXERS

A multiplexer allows:

- Sharing of a single high-speed/high-volume transmission line among several users.
- Reductions in the number of transmission links by directing traffic to a higher bandwidth link.
- Reductions in overall communications costs.
- Configuration of diverse network topologies such as point-to-point, ring, tree, or hub.

SONET multiplexers come in two varieties—a terminal concentrator type with many-to-one and one-to-many multiplexing/demultiplexing, and a new type of add/drop multiplexer (ADM). Both types convert between electrical and optical signal environments. Internally, SONET multiplexers propagate STS-1 and STS-3 electrical signals for DSN mapping, interconnecting, and distribution at the local site, and multiplex them to form higher-rate STS-n and OC-n signals. In an ADM multiplexer, the incoming and outgoing signals are at identical rates, while the lower-speed signals are dropped and added to it (Figure 8.1). The ADM allows lower-rate signals to be groomed from incoming signals and added to outgoing higher-rate signals. Nonterminating signals pass through transparently from one port to another. Both TM and ADM multiplexers have a rich selection of interfaces and features that permit configuration of simple as well as complex SONET networks.

8.2.1. Interfaces

SONET multiplexers are compatible with the existing telecom infrastructure because they support asynchronous as well as synchronous electrical interfaces for DS1, DS1c, DS2, and DS3 signals—and their mapping into the corresponding VT1.5, VT3, VT6 and STS-1 payloads. The DS1 is the most widely used interface and is available in almost all SONET multiplexers. High-speed optical OC-n signals are provisioned on a selective basis where n = 1,3,9,12,18,24,36, and 48. The actual multiplexer data rate depends upon whether it is deployed in a high- or low-traffic area (Table 8.1). In inner cities, where bulk transmission is crucial, OC-12, OC-24, and OC-48 rates will dominate the network transport. Likewise, OC-3, OC-12, and OC-24 rates provide adequate capacity for feeder applications. In suburban areas, OC-3 and OC-12 would be adequate to meet the traffic needs either in transport or feeder sections. OC-1 and OC-3 will be adequate for rural areas.

8.2.2. Features

SONET multiplexers offer a wide selection of features:

- Direct termination of OC-n signals, where n = 1, 3, 9, 12, 18, 24, 36, and 48.
- Termination of low-speed clear channel DSn signals.
- Multiplexing/demultiplexing of DSn signals from/to OC-n ports. The multiplexer uses a floating VT mapping structure for DS1, DS1c, and DS2, while DS3 signals are mapped directly into STS-1s.
- Add/Drop of DSn signals from an OC-n pipe, which gives SONET networking its unique capability. The signals are either dropped when traveling in the downstream direction and added upstream, or dropped from upstream signals and added downstream. Unaffected signals are simply passed.
- Remote and local operations interface to operations, administrations, maintenance, and provisioning. The EOC is the conduit for management commands.
- *Additional features include* VT add/drop, VT locked-mode operation, STS-1 add/drop, DS3 SYNTRAN mapping, ring applications with automatic protection switching (APS), loop-back capability for access, test, and in-service rolling.

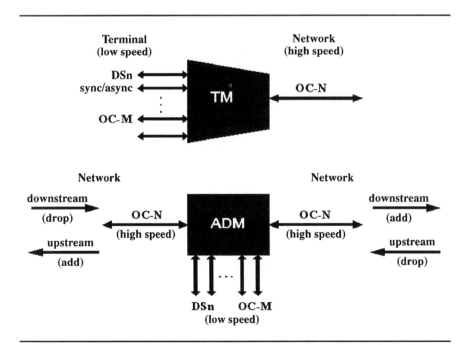

Figure 8.1.   Conceptual difference between TM and ADM.

Table 8.1.　　Predominant rates for NEs vs. Serving Areas.

	multiplexers transport feeder		RFTs access only	WDCS transport only	BDCS transport only
inner city	OC–12	OC–3	OC–3	OC–3	OC–12
	OC–24	OC–12	OC–12	OC–12	OC–24
	OC–48	OC–24		OC–24	OC–48
				OC–48	
suburban	OC–3	OC–3	OC–1	OC–3	OC–12
	OC–12	OC–12	OC–3	OC–12	OC–24
rural	OC–1	OC–1	OC–1	OC–1	OC–12
	OC–3	OC–3	OC–3	OC–3	

8.2.3.　Ring Applications

ADMs may be interconnected to form a ring (Figure 8.2). For path protection switching (PPS), two unidirectional fiber pairs are used between ADMs to back each other up in the event of a single fiber failure. In a dual ring structure, two separate fiber rings are used. Each ADM on the ring transmits and receives simultaneously. Both fibers are monitored but only one is used by the ADM. Thus a single fiber failure is serviced by switching to the second.

8.3.　REMOTE FIBER TERMINAL (RFT)

The application of remote fiber terminals (RFTs) into the loop and distribution network transcends a long history in wire technology. Historically, miles of twisted copper pairs bundled together served as access and feeder sections at the same time. One pair of copper wires was dedicated to voice or POTS traffic, all the way from the customer's premises to the central office. In the 1960's, analog loop carrier (ALC) systems evolved to provide pair gain in the local loop or access network, while T1 digital technology became available for interoffice traffic. AT&T's SLC 96 systems in 1979 introduced digital technology to the loop. SLC 96 concentrates 24 POTS lines or channels over a single T1 line. Four T1 lines serve 96 subscribers, and a fifth T1 line provides protection switching. The SLC 96 or universal digital loop carriers (UDLC) were never in-

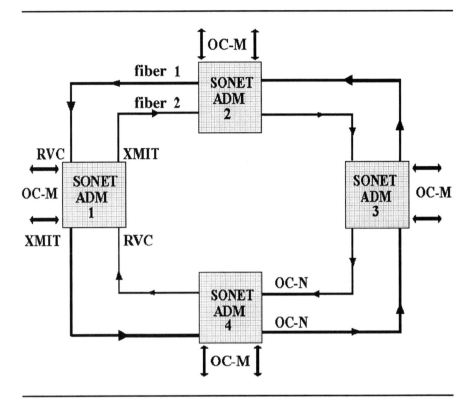

Figure 8.2.   Dual ring/unidirectional structure.

tended as long term solutions. Because UDLC accommodates and interfaces with all types of switches—SPC, mechanical, analog, and digital—
design compromises were made that limit performance. Nonetheless,
digital technology in the loop was shown to make economic sense and
work began on more advanced versions.

During the 1980's, Bellcore defined an all-digital DS1-based loop
system called integrated digital loop carrier (IDLC-TR303) to interface
with a digital CO. In the late 1980's, a migration strategy to fiber in the
loop (FITL) with SONET standards was defined by Bellcore as a supple-
ment to the IDLC and TR303. Today, SONET has emerged as a physical layer alternative for loop plant as well. All remote digital terminals
(RDTs or RFTs) are SONET-compatible. Deploying SONET in the local
loop provides:

- Consistency of interfaces and standards in the access section with those in the feeder and transport sections.
- Replacement of millions of copper cable miles with bandwidth-rich fiber. This will be expensive, but will improve transmission and reliability. New services will provide significant revenues.

A remote terminal with a fiber interface provides a fully digital path from customer premises back to the central office, and more. It provides an end-to-end fiber path with a full SONET capacity. On business premises, the RFT provides both narrowband (64 Kb/s) and wideband (DS1-1.5 Mb/s to DS3-45 Mb/s) interfaces directly off the RFT cabinet (Figure 8.3). In this scenario, the entire loop from the business premises to the CO will be digital.

Due to its lower density, the residential network section today uses a different topology. Fiber is being extended from the RFTs to the opti-

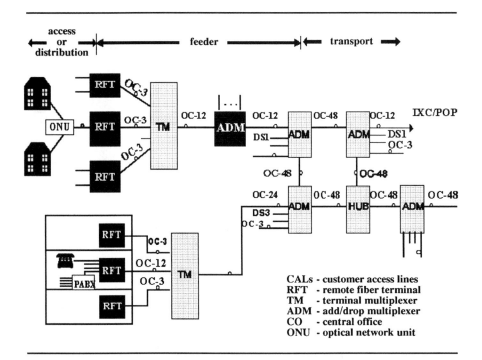

Figure 8.3. SONET network.

cal network units (ONUs), then copper pairs go into homes. In the future, the copper pairs will be replaced with fiber as demand for new broadband services increases.

8.4.   DIGITAL CROSSCONNECT (DCS)

Like multiplexers, digital cross-connects serve many purposes. They:

* Terminate digital signals and facilities
* Cross-connect same-level signals automatically
* Cross-connect constituent (tributary) signals automatically
* Provide transparent grooming and routing
* Optimize use of network elements and facilities
* Allow hubbing and network management capability
* Reduce provisioning and administrative costs

There are two types of SONET DCSs—a wideband type (WDCS) and the broadband type, or BDCS. Wideband DCS is limited to DS1s/VT1.5s. In the cross-connect process, the wideband DCS terminates the incoming DS1, DS3 and OC-n incoming signals and generates new frames for outgoing signals. The B DCSs perform DS3/STS-1 and STS3c to STS3c cross-connection by terminating both DS3 and OC-n signals. The cross-connect function is closer to switching than multiplexing. SONET brings a variety of signals to the CO. There is the opportunity to perform more and more low-level crossconnecting within the CO. This will happen. With fewer higher-level signals to be cross-connected outside the CO, wideband as well as broadband functionality can be combined optimally in a single system (Figure 8.4).

8.4.1.   Interfaces

SONET DCSs provide both asynchronous and synchronous electrical interfaces for DS1 and DS3 signals. The OC-n optical signals are provisioned on a selective basis. For wideband cross-connect operations, OC-1, OC-3, OC-12, and OC-24 provide a reasonable mix of port sizes to combine hubbing, interoffice transport, and DS1/VT1.5 cross-connect. Broadband DCS uses the higher rates offered by OC-12, OC-24, and OC-48, as well as STS-1 and STS-3 electrical signal. These are used for DS1/DS3 mapping and cross-connecting to VT1.5/STS-1 respectively, STS-3c/STS3c cross-connecting, and for intra-office equipment interconnection.

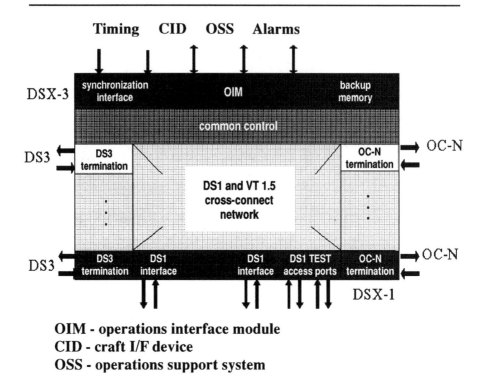

Figure 8.4.   SONET Cross-connect structure.

8.4.2. DCS Features

Wideband cross-connect system functions include:

- Providing a low-speed DS1 clear channel interface to cross-connect DS1 to DS1, DS3, or floating VT1.5. The transparent cross-connection includes a framing bit (F Bit), ABCD coding, CRC6, yellow AIS, and the ESF data link.
- Terminating incoming asynchronous DS3 signals and generating new frames for outgoing signals. Cross-connect constituent DS1s to different outgoing signals DS1, DS3, or VT1.5.
- Terminating the incoming OC-n and generating new frames for outgoing signals, and at the same time processing STS-1 overhead

and frame alignment. Constituent VT1.5s are cross-connected to different outgoing signals (Table 8.2).

- Provide an interface for operations, administration, maintenance, and provisioning functions that include memory and database administration, performance monitoring, alarm surveillance, and signal facility maintenance with loop-back.
- Additional features may include enhanced DS1 performance monitoring, APS, in-service rolling, DS1 broadcast, side-door port for bypass, downloadable software generics, VT2, VT3, and VT6 cross-connection, and more.

Broadband cross-connect system functions include:

- DS3 clear-channel interface for both asynchronous and synchronous signals, which provides cross-connection of DS3 to another DS3, STS-1 (OC-n), or itself for loop-back.
- Terminates an OC-n signal while constituent STS-1s and STS3cs perform cross-connect functions. STS-1s may cross-connect to DS3s, another STS-1 within the same OC-n, or to itself for loop-back. STS-3cs only cross-connect with STS-3c or to itself for loop-back function.
- Provides an operations interface for operations, administration, maintenance, and provisioning functions that is similar to those in WDCS.
- Additional features include broadcast capability (useful in video services), enhanced DS3 performance monitoring, automatic protection switching (APS), in-service rolling, downloadable software generics, and others.

Table 8.2.   Cross-connect signal matrix.

floating VT1.5	floating VT1.5				
	async DS3	DS1 CC	async	bit sync	byte sync
async DS3	Y	Y	Y	N	N
DS1 CC	Y	Y	Y	N	N
async	Y	Y	Y	N	N
bit sync	N	N	N	Y	N
byte sync	N	N	N	N	Y

8.5. SWITCHING

Some manufacturers have gone beyond simple, stand-alone SONET network elements and have integrated switches. The cross-connect functions may be integrated within the switch element or be an adjunct to the switch and only perform a cross-connect as part of the CO-hub (Figure 8.5). SONET technology within the switch is important because it:

- Meets demands of customers for higher bandwidth and new dial-up services.
- Automates operations, administration, maintenance and provisioning processes and reduces network engineering costs.
- Gives network providers fully integrated network elements to build a platform that will offer new services rapidly and flexibly.

The marriage of SONET and switching systems will bring about a dramatic change in the wire center (Figure 8.6). SONET will simplify the network by replacing thousands of copper cables with a single-fiber cable system and eliminate redundant equipment, starting with main distribution frame (MDF), digital signal cross-connect frame (DSX) patch panels, channel banks, stand-alone fiber optic terminals (FOTs), M13 multiplexers, and stand-alone 3 one/zero cross-connects.

8.6. ASYNCHRONOUS EQUIPMENT COMPATIBILITY

SONET network elements ensure compatibility with the existing telecommunications network. Interfaces with the current telecommunications components such as transmission system, outside plant fiber, operations systems, and power systems, are part of the SONET standards. It is possible to interconnect SONET equipment at the standard hierarchical cross-connects such as DSX-1, DSX-1C, DSX-2, DSX-3, and DSX-4NA. In addition, SONET NEs provide electrical interfaces at STSX-1 and STSX-3 for SONET cross-connect facilities. It is, however, necessary to pay attention to the length of interconnecting cables, otherwise timing problems and related alarms may occur (Table 8.3). The maximum cable distance between the terminal and the cross-connect frame should not exceed the lengths in the table.

Furthermore, SONET NE's interact with maintenance signals of the existing hierarchical rates (DS-1, DS-1C, DS-3, DS-4NA). SONET propagates the corresponding maintenance signals within the STS fabric, and vice versa, using VTs. So the old 'DS' maintenance signals and the new SONET maintenance signals are fully compatible. Moreover,

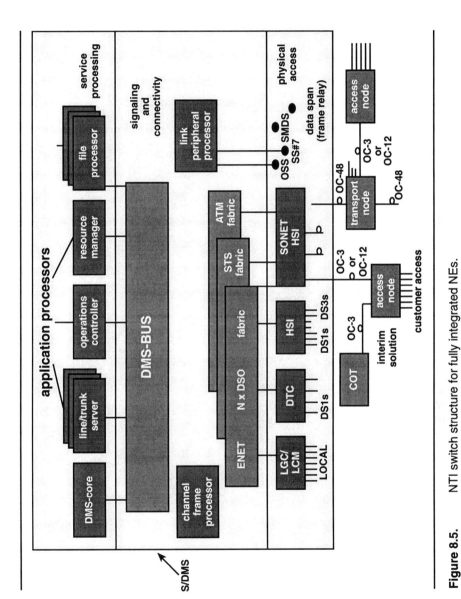

Figure 8.5. NTI switch structure for fully integrated NEs.

125

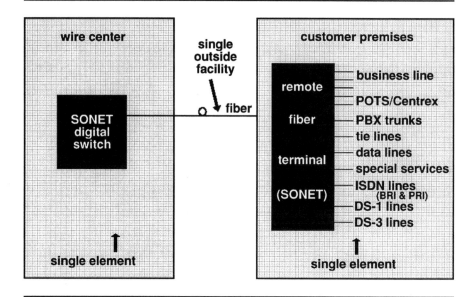

Figure 8.6. SONET-based access.

fiber distributing frames and optical DSXs connect any fiber cable to any regenerator without disassembling splices. The number of terminations and the type of fiber cable connections will further determine compatibility. SONET does not impose any new requirements for the mechanical interconnection of the fiber cables. The issue of mechanical compatibility for physical connections to SONET equipment is the same as that with the non-SONET fiber equipment.

Table 8.3. Maximum terminal and cross-connect frame distance (in feet)

cross-connect frame	maximum cable distance
DSX-1 and DSX-1C	655
DSX-2	1000
DSX-3 and STSX-1	450
DSX-4NA and STSX-3	225

8.7.   APPLICATIONS

Today's asynchronous public telephone network uses a mix of manual patch panels, stand-alone digital cross-connect systems, and T1/T3 multiplexers to provide access and bandwidth management for new Telco/PTT services. The network elements are deployed at key locations to handle line and trunk grooming, cross-connecting, multiplexing, and demultiplexing. In Telco/PTT networks, CO-hubs consisting of manually adjusted MDFs, channel banks, customer access line blocks, stand-alone fiber terminals, trunking blocks, etc., along with local tandems and access tandems, are all interconnected (Figure 8.7). These network elements limit the capacity of the public telephone network for on-demand bandwidth services.

In contrast, SONET eliminates the need for external MDFs and DSX patch panels. It does away with channel banks, FOTs, and M13 multiplexers to provide more elegant and simpler networking solutions.

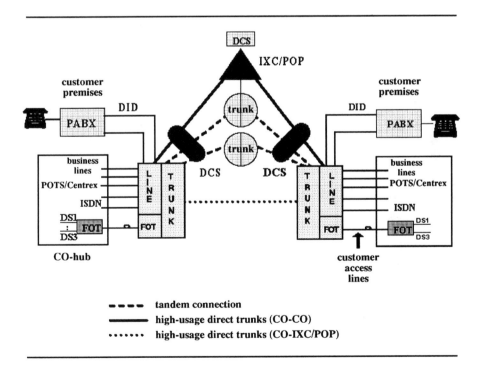

Figure 8.7.   Today's networking scenario.

SONET collapses the myriad of network elements into three primary elements; ADM/TM multiplexers, remote fiber terminals (RFTs) and digital cross-connects. These are specialized to operate in the access or distribution, feeder, and transport sections of the public telephone network. SONET multiplexers (ADMs and TMs) are used in both the transport and feeder sections; RFTs make up the bulk of the access or distribution section. In residential areas, deployment of optical network units (ONUs) is already underway. The digital cross-connect systems that provide grooming and service expansion functions are part of the SONET CO-hub. These hubs primarily perform switching at rates that depend on the section of the network in which they are deployed.

8.7.1. Self-healing Ring Structures

Fiber rings are being deployed in business districts of major cities in the United States (such as Cincinnati). Both local exchange carriers and alternate local transport companies are pursuing ring deployments vigorously. These rings are made 'self-healing' by incorporating automatic switching, which selects the secondary source of traffic in the event of a cable cut. Thus a single point of failure cannot stop two locations on the ring from communicating. This high survivability emphasizes the critical importance of communication links to business operations. The initial focus of survivable circuits was on the crucial, high-volume trunks linking Telco central offices with interexchange carrier points of presence. This was extended to alternate central office access links. Beyond the central business districts, self-healing fiber networks are reaching to the surrounding industrial parks and suburban business locations.

SONET technology facilitates the creation of fiber ring structures and greatly enhances their functionality and economical operation. Indeed, some Telco/PTTs have indicated that their interest in SONET is almost solely based on obtaining add/drop multiplexer capability that facilitates the insertion and extraction of traffic into survivable fiber rings.

8.7.1.1. Dual Ring/Unidirectional Structure. Ring structures consisting of two fibers, one as a working path and the other its backup, are most suited for collecting, routing, transporting, and distributing traffic, especially with the add/drop functionality of SONET multiplexers (Figure 8.8). The total OC-N ring bandwidth is shared by all the nodes in the ring. A SONET ADM, DCS, or any other functionally equivalent network element may be employed, although in most ring applications the ADM provides the best fit. Both fiber cables carry the same traffic, but in opposite directions. One fiber is the working or active fiber, while the other is

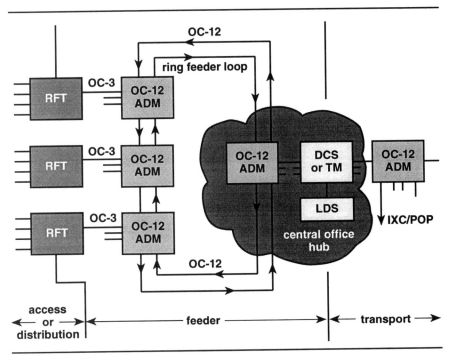

Figure 8.8.   SONET suburban ring-based network.

the back up. Each node in the ring simultaneously transmits, receives, and monitors the two opposing paths. During normal operation, the node selects the working fiber signal for STS/VT processing and handling. In the event of a fiber failure, a path-failed alarm signal is propagated downstream to all nodes. Since the downstream node monitors both fiber signals, it selects the path that has a valid signal, in this case, the signal from the backup fiber. Thus the dual-ring structure offers an alternate signal that is identified and selected by individual nodes in the event of a single fiber failure. At least two consecutive failures of the fiber transmission path must occur to disrupt service to any given customer location— a highly unlikely event.

8.7.1.2. Interoffice Ring.   The SONET ring may interconnect central offices and provide a very reliable and flexible DS3/DS1 path between COs (Figure 8.9). The OC-N capacity of the ring accommodates the DS3/DS1 bandwidth needs of the three COs and the hub office.

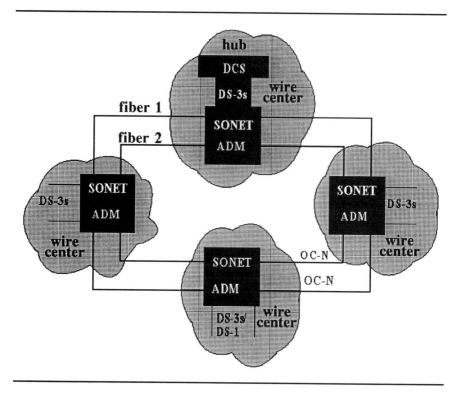

Figure 8.9.   Interoffice ring applications.

Since all the ring traffic is not processed at the hub, a smaller DCS may suffice to handle the outside traffic homing on the hub office. This reflects one advantage of a SONET ring, in that bandwidth capacity can be changed simply by adding higher- or lower-rate network elements: all segments of the ring do not need the same capacity. For additional bulk DS3 traffic between two COs, a separate but direct CO-to-CO fiber system could be established with its own line protection switching. The ring would be off-loaded and the available bandwidth used to support the traffic growth of other CO pairs.

8.7.1.3. Loop (Feeder) Ring.   The use of ring structures in the access loop or the network feeder section simplifies the process of traffic collection and distribution. As shown in Figure 8.10, three RFTs communi-

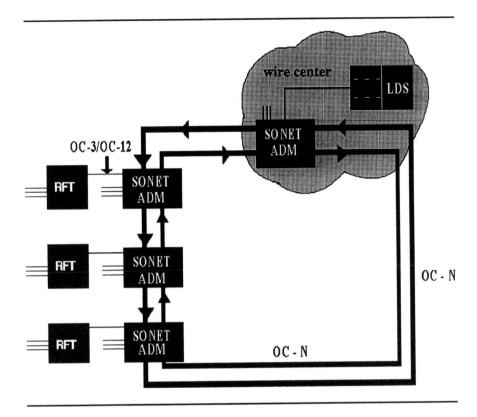

Figure 8.10. Loop (Feeder) ring application.

cate with the local digital switch, using SONET ADMs interconnected in a ring. The SONET ADMs that collect and route traffic to the central office also pick up traffic that originates at the RFTs. The RFTs connect to the SONET ADM over an OC-3 or OC-12 fiber link, depending on customer service demands.

8.7.1.4. Hierarchical Rings. Geographic considerations, as well as bandwidth management, may dictate that a network be constructed from multiple, interconnected rings. A multi ring topology segregates traffic—an interoffice ring can carry STS traffic while an access ring carries VT traffic. From the point of presence (POP) in Figure 8.11, STS-1 signals from an interexchange carrier are carried on the interof-

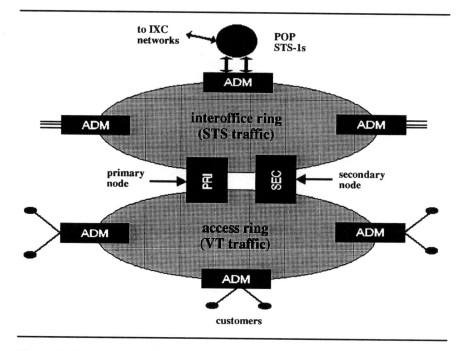

Figure 8.11.   Hierarchical multi ring structure.

fice ring to the serving node and terminated. DS3s are terminated by the SONET ADMs at the POP, and from there are transported within an STS-1 signal on the interoffice ring. The DS3s are processed by serving nodes attached to the interoffice ring. The demultiplexing of the STS-1 signals into VTs/DS1s, and the routing of VT/DS1s to the access ring, is accomplished at the primary and secondary serving nodes. The serving nodes in the access ring terminate VT/DS1s as appropriate. Similarly, VT traffic from customers on the access ring is routed via the nodes onto the interoffice ring and then to the POP.

Both the interoffice and access rings function independently, with primary and secondary nodes coordinating operations between the two rings and satisfying the dual-ring, unidirectional transmission. Service is unaffected either by a primary or secondary node failure, or by simultaneous single failure in both rings. Furthermore, a failure in one ring has no effect on the operation of the other. This robustness makes the multi ring an excellent choice for use in interoffice as well as loop applications.

8.8. RESEARCH NETWORKS

Applications of gigabit per second networks are being tested in five separate networking testbeds supported by the Corporation for National Research Initiatives (CNRI), the National Science Foundation (NSF), the Defense Advanced Research Projects Agency (DARPA), and participating long-distance carriers, regional telephone companies, and switch vendors. The testbeds all use SONET transmission backbone at 2.488 Gb/s, and 622 Mb/s channels. Each project focuses on a different aspect of high-speed networking and computing:

- *Multimedia*—The Aurora project compares two networks: one for ATM over SONET using BellCore prototype switching equipment; another for variable-length packet-switching called packet transfer mode (PTM). PTM uses IBM's experimental Planet switch. .
- *High-speed network control*—The Blanca project connects two networks over a transcontinental T3 line. Research is focused on real-time protocols for control and transport of remote images, as well as their visualization and simulation.
- *Distributed computer computation*—The Casa project connects high performance parallel interface (HIPPI) directly over SONET to investigate parallel computing.
- *High-speed data delivery*—The Nectar project investigates the impact of the full 2.488 Gb/s bandwidth to a single end-point. A general gateway from a local area HIPPI network to ATM over a 30 km SONET link is being developed.
- *Distributed high-speed networks*—The Vistanet project links a HIPPI LAN to the ATM over SONET WAN. A major focus is medical imaging.

Having computers successfully accept data at 622 Mb/s and higher rates is a common problem encountered by the research networks. Computer operating systems that support such high rates need to be developed. This research should continue for several years and lead to a better understanding of the interaction between broadband networks and attached computers.

8.9. BYPASS AND DARK FIBER

Recognizing the considerable investment required by embedded asynchronous equipment, the telephone companies will be slow to replace perfectly usable existing equipment. At issue is when to begin the upgrade. The North American and European digital transmission rates fall below those of their SONET counterparts. Although SONET NEs support the major existing framing formats, the reverse is not true. It is not possible to cram SONET signals into the existing network. Pressure from private networks will act as a catalyst to SONET deployment. Within the confines of the corporation, the seeds of SONET are sprouting. These sprouts could force the telephone companies into deploying SONET earlier than planned. Corporations are choosing either dark fiber routing or bypass providers if the telephone company is unwilling to co-locate SONET equipment at the CO.

The issue of dark fiber dates back to the mid-1980s, when the local telephone companies installed dark fiber as the foundation for high-speed point-to-point links in private user networks. The telephone companies supplied the fiber optic lines, and the electronics that were attached for a DS0 in the 1980s could be replaced with SONET gear that supports an OC-3 (155 Mb/s) line today. The telephone companies initially offered the fiber on an individual case basis. That is, they worked out a method with users to cover the cost of purchasing, installing and maintaining the fiber. But when the FCC in the 1990s decided that formal tariffs were required for the service, the carriers tried to exit the service as user demand was increasing.

There will be situations where the telephone company takes the initiative, because the service and bandwidth requirements can only be satisfied with new SONET NEs. New installations will also favor SONET. But the deployment of SONET begins in a network environment dominated by asynchronous multiplexing of the DS N hierarchy. Existing asynchronous multiplexers and SONET NEs will coexist in the same network—at least in the near future. Therefore, there will be no wide-scale replacement of DS 3 networks, but rather a gradual overlayment by SONET equipment. Thus, any general application needs to be studied three ways; the existing network solution, the temporary hybrid solution, and the pure SONET solution.

8.10. CONCLUSION

SONET has the promise of bringing public and private networks together with a common equipment and control format that makes sense in both environments. It provides a variety of network topologies to select from. The most desirable network topology will vary, depending on the speed of SONET migration into the public network. SONET supports the current asynchronous signals, but the reverse is not true, necessitating a transition period in which isolated SONET network islands will be deployed with current asynchronous broadband networks, until pure SONET implementations become the norm.

9

MANs to WANs

9.1. INTRODUCTION

Business survival depends on access to the right information at the right time, which in turn allows the mobilization of proper responses to customers, competition, and opportunities. The current trend toward corporate downsizing and moving staff closer to the customer has resulted in global enterprise dispersion. This phenomenon has created the need to interconnect millions of local computer environments. According to *Telecommunications Magazine*, more than 60% of U.S. companies are actively engaged in interconnecting LANs. Even more are concerned with communications between dissimilar mainframes, minicomputers, and other office automation vehicles. Broadband networking is being driven by many forces, and principal among them is the increasing need among LAN users for high-speed data services. Two trends are responsible for multimegabit data communications:

- The need to interconnect traditional LANs over an even higher-capacity backbone LAN.
- The dramatic increase in computing power, and the equally dramatic decline in its cost. (See Figure 2.1.)

One result of these trends is a bewildering—and continuously developing—array of new carrier services that seamlessly internetwork LANs and WANs, satisfying the demand for sophisticated data, image, and video communications (Table 9.1). Emerging services include switched multimegabit data service (SMDS) offered by the Telco/PTT, and BISDN/ATM offered by LAN equipment vendors *and* Telco/PTT. They are dependent upon newly emerging technologies. SONET/SDH forms the basis for linking high-speed LANs, while ATM realizes the full potential of bandwidth-on-demand services. Together they integrate LAN and WAN network elements, using common equipment and signaling, making possible a rich variety of network architectures.

This section describes the types of broadband networks presently being implemented. These networks are not growing up in a vacuum. Emerging applications continue to fuel the demand for broadband equipment and services. Consider the value of having hospitals globally linked: patients will have access to the best doctors and diagnostic routines no matter where they are located. For example, doctors in Los Angeles could use a software program to discover and explore anomalies in a patient located in Moscow. Magnetic resonance images could be evaluated in real-time by a supercomputer, eliminating hours, even days, of processing delay.

This situation has encouraged the growth of distributed networks whose resources are shared by many users or dedicated to specific users as needs may warrant. The demand among businesses for distributed processing and high-speed networking, unconstrained by geographical limitations, can only be fulfilled by the emerging broadband network hierarchy. But instead of connecting from the LAN into the broadband WAN directly, a new form of intermediary is being deployed—the metropolitan area network (MAN) (Figure 9.1). Its purpose is twofold: first,

Table 9.1. Advanced network services projection.

Service	1993 share of total revenues	1998 share of total revenues	2003 share of total revenues
frame relay	94%	38%	1%
SMDS	5%	37%	4%
ATM	1%	24%	60%
broadband ISDN	—	1%	35%
total	$ 696 million	$26 billion	$ 138 billion

Source: Electronicast Corp., San Matco, California

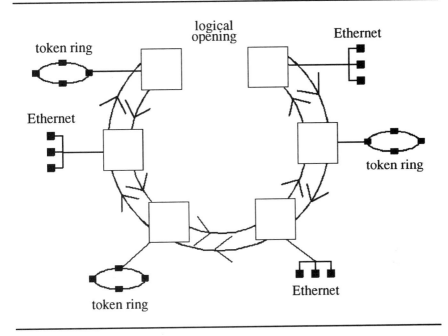

Figure 9.1.   Metropolitan Area Network (MAN).

to provide a regional conduit for broadband traffic; second, to gather information in volumes that warrant the economical connection to the broadband WAN. The MAN comes in many forms, both proprietary and standard. Its most popular form is SMDS.

9.2.   SWITCHED MULTIMEGABIT DATA SERVICE (SMDS)

SMDS is a specification for a metropolitan area, high-speed data service distributed by Regional Bell Operating Companies (RBOCs). SMDS allows the same type of connectivity for data that the telephone offers for voice and fax. Information is transported over counter-rotating rings that extend over a municipality. Users gain switched access to a network that provides:

• A high-speed data service within a metropolitan area.
• Features similar to those found in LANs; in particular, high bandwidth and low delay.

- Easy integration with existing systems and the capacity to evolve gracefully with them.
- Security features, such as closed user groups.
- A connectionless, high-speed packet service.

The needs for MAN services, and for SMDS in particular, are quite varied. Any data transfer requiring high speeds, such as imaging, computer-aided design, publishing, and financial applications, can benefit from SMDS. Data packets of up to 9188 octets can be transferred across an SMDS network, distributed queue dual bus operating over an underlying dual bus (DQDB) subnetwork. DQDB is an IEEE cell-relay network standard, switching and transmitting 53-byte cells. These cells have the same format as those defined in ATM and BISDN standards. Thus, DQDB delivers a compatible format to carry SMDS data and interoperate with emerging networks that are accessed across a dedicated link, typically from a customer's network. According to current specifications, access will be by means of a DS1 or DS3 line, with service classes defined for a sustained transfer rate of four, 10, 16, 25, and 34 Mb/s. A SONET/SDH interface at STS-3/STM-1 is expected in the future.

SMDS is aimed at companies with the following basic profile:

- Multiple, geographically dispersed locations, each with its own LAN and/or host computer system.
- A need to exchange information among locations or with other businesses.
- An expected growth in data traffic that will require a high-speed backbone with greater capacity than is currently available or affordable.
- A preference for a public network rather than a private one.

SMDS was conceived as a high-speed public packet service, mainly to interconnect local area networks. Like any LAN, SMDS requires an access technique to prevent overlapping transmissions. Unlike LANs that use either CSMA/CD or token passing techniques, SMDS uses a distributed reservation scheme in which each node keeps count of the access requests made by the nodes ahead of it. Like all LAN protocols, SMDS is connectionless—it does not set up the sequence that has become known as a virtual circuit. Each packet or datagram is addressed and switched independently, with no prior network connection. But public SMDS packet switches will have to deal with multiple connections and are likely to use virtual circuits to transmit data.

Each SMDS packet has the capacity for as many as 9188 bytes of data, which allows SMDS to accommodate entire packets from most LANs—Ethernet and token ring, with the exception of 16 Mb/s token ring which can have a maximum frame size of 16,000 bytes, and all 100 Mb/s FDDIs. Furthermore, the packets of SMDS are divided into cells or slots of fixed length—53 bytes per cell, of which 48 contain data and five are for control. The lower layers of SMDS interface protocol (SIP) transmit 53-byte cells, or *slots*, which is also consistent with the ATM structure.

In 1991, a consortium of internetworking and wide area network vendors proposed an SMDS interface (Figure 9.2). The interface is designed to enable routers supporting LANs to connect to SMDS networks via data service unit/channel service units, or DSU/CSUs. Also, the interface partitions SMDS functions between the router and the DSU/CSU. This interface is based on a high-level data link control (HLDC) protocol

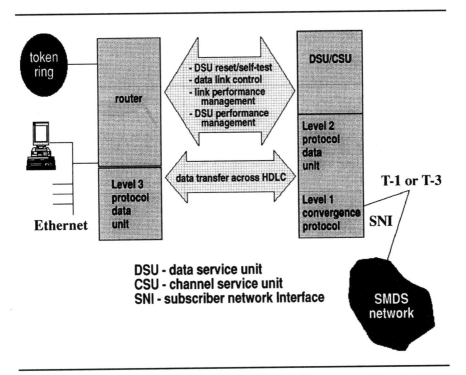

Figure 9.2.   Proposed SMDS interface.

which is widely used for communications between LAN and DSU/CSU equipment.

In a MAN configuration, SMDS can interconnect users for distances of up to 50 kilometers. Beyond that, interconnection by means of a SONET-WAN is desirable, with DS3-based networking as an alternative (Figure 9.3). For users to communicate over the SONET-WAN from one SMDS/MAN to another requires a gateway or bridging function. The bridge/router may do the DS1/DS3 signal mapping to SONET VT1.5/ STS-1 subsequent to a SONET NE interface. The SONET NE would provide DS1/DS3/OC-1/OC-3 extensions as required.

9.3. WANs

As a high-speed data transport, the public telephone network is running out of gas because it was originally designed for voice traffic and only recently has seen the balance of traffic shift to data. Under the assault of new data applications emanating from LANs, asynchronous network elements are failing to meet the need for higher-speed and better-managed information highways. The solution is the intelligent broadband network that uses SONET/SDH transport and ATM switch-

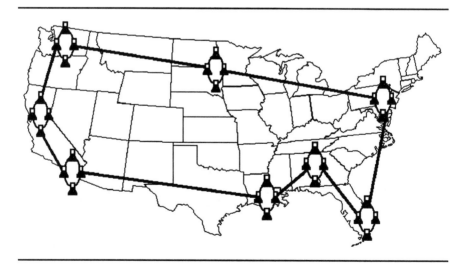

Figure 9.3.   MAN internet.

ing to create, in the coming decade, ever-faster information superhigh-ways (Figure 9.4). Fortunately, technological advances and decreasing hardware costs favor the creation of broadband network elements that incorporate the best features of public and private network equipment.

9.3.1. Broadband WAN Elements

The network elements described in this section form the basic building blocks for networks, whether public or private.

9.3.1.1. Router. The router provides protocol conversion between LAN packets and broadband wide area networks. For example, a router will convert between LAN frames and ATM cells transmitted over an ATM-switched network. A segmentation and reassembly (SAR) function within such a router will implement an AAL to convert LAN frames into cells for transmission, and reassemble received ATM cells into LAN frames. Eventually this capability will allow ATM to be used for high-speed 'backbone' transmission of LAN and WAN traffic, while individual users maintain their existing LAN standards and cost structure.

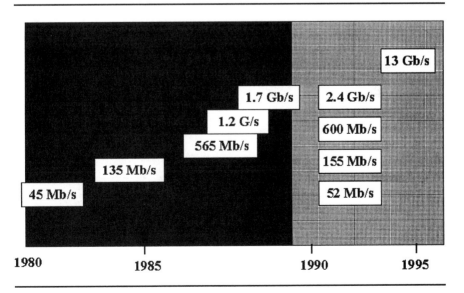

Figure 9.4.   Increasing network speeds.

9.3.1.2. Switch. The public network switch is a larger, more intelligent version of the enterprise switch. A public switch is capable of handling hundreds of thousands of cells per second and has thousands of switch ports, each operating at SONET/SDH rates (Figure 9.5). All cell processing functions are performed by the input controllers and the switching fabric. In a broadband switch, cell arrivals are not scheduled. The switch takes all incoming packets, divides them into 53-byte cells, adds headers and then retransmits them onto the network. If SONET/SDH is used, the available bandwidth has already been divided into slots (Figure 9.6). The control processor resolves contentions when they occur, as well as call set up and tear down, bandwidth reservation, maintenance, and management. The input/output (I/O) ports are synchronized so that all cells arrive at the switch fabric with their headers aligned. The resulting traffic is said to be *slotted,* and the time to transmit a cell across the switch fabric is called a *timeslot.* All VCIs are translated in the input controllers. Each incoming VCI is funneled into the proper output port as defined in a routing table. At the I/O ports, the cells are formatted in the proper transmission format. For example, a broadband ISDN port provides a line terminator to handle the physical level transmission, and an exchange terminator for cell processing.

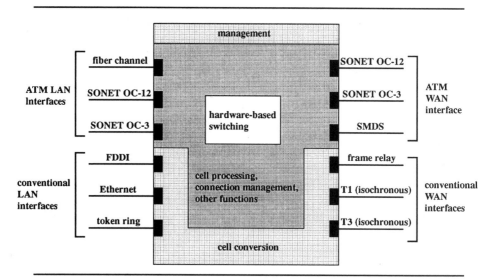

Figure 9.5.   Broadband switch.

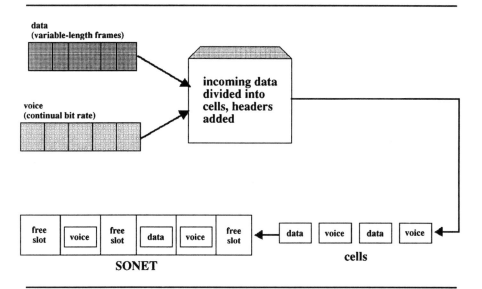

Figure 9.6.   Broadband switching.

9.3.1.3. Multiplexer.   The slowest defined data rate for broadband networks is faster than that at which most routers, bridges and video CODer/DEcoders (Codecs) operate. Even at T1 rates, a time division multiplexer (TDM) is used to share the bandwidth. It switches among the 24 channels, interleaving the bits into one continuous digital stream of 1.544 Mb/s. Multiplexing is done in pairs. At the source, a multiplexer interleaves the bits from various sources, while a multiplexer at the destination separates the bit stream into the 24 channels. At higher data rates, multiplexing becomes even more important. The network manager has the choice of dedicating a high-capacity circuit to each low-speed device, possibly wasting bandwidth, or multiplexing several lower-speed signals onto a broadband circuit. A broadband multiplexer may be considered similar to a switch, but it does more than just provide connectivity to multiple users: it handles isochronous data such as voice and video. The multiplexer accepts data from routers and bridges through a standard interface (V.35 or HSSI), segments the data into cells, addresses each cell, and maps the cells into a WAN framing structure (T3/E3 or SONET/SDH).

9.3.1.4. CSU/DSU. The purpose of the CSU/DSU is to encapsulate information into the proper framing before it enters the WAN. The CSU/DSU converts between communications technologies by providing the interface between the on-site hub, switch, or router formats, and the broadband network. The CSU/DSU regenerates the signals received from the network and can also serve as a way to troubleshoot the transmission line. The CSU/DSU automatically monitors the signal to detect violations and signal loss. When problems are detected, it allows remote network testing from the central office, including loop-back testing of the transmission line.

9.4. FRAME RELAY NETWORKS

Communications systems that hold the line open, empty, and waiting for the next burst of information, force users to pay for more bandwidth than they need. Packet-switching networks allow for the much more economical transmission of computer data. The X.25 protocol commonly used in packet-switched networks transports a standard amount of data packaged with an address. When a data packet arrives at a node, the node checks for errors and, if it finds none, reads the packet's address and routes it accordingly. Packets arriving at their destination are assembled by the receiver. The benefit of X.25 packet-switching is that messages for many different destinations can share the same transmission facilities at any given time.

Frame relay is this generation's technology alternative to older, slower transport networks such as X.25 and synchronous data link control (SDLC). Some experts predict that users could increase throughput by 30 to 50% by running SNA traffic over frame relay rather than SDLC. A public frame relay network is a multinode network of switches with dedicated connections to customer sites (Figure 9.7). Frame relay is often the access protocol into the network switch. Different protocols may be employed between switches. The service provider allows access to its switch by means of DS0 and T1 lines. These leased lines have a fixed rate that is prenegotiated with the carrier. As these customer-to-POP lines are relatively short, their rental costs are small and the customer's traffic is aggregated with others to save in long-haul transport costs. The attractiveness of frame relay services to users is their cost-effectiveness. The services can interface with existing customer hardware at a minimum upgrade cost, and may be optimized for transporting bursts of traffic characteristic of LAN internets. Customers are charged for the number of permanent virtual circuits (PVCs) and connected end-points. The PVC data rate is the committed information

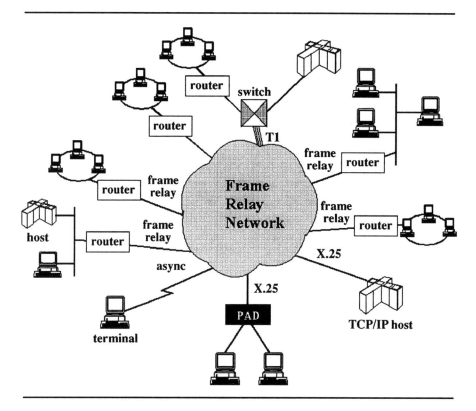

Figure 9.7.   Frame relay network.

rate (CIR), which is the maximum average data rate of each PVC. This rate can be exceeded during bursts of LAN traffic, which is advantageous to users.

Frame relay networks provide:

* Efficient accommodation of bursty applications that require high-speed data transport.
* Cost-effective alternatives to leased lines, especially for full logical mesh connectivity.
* ANSI- and CCITT-approved standards-based infrastructure.
* Support for the interconnection of LANs running different protocols.

The applications that frame relay can support are limited. Lower-speed applications will be satisfied, but others will have to wait for faster networks such as ATM. For example, the need to define PVCs between devices is well suited to SDLC, where users are accustomed to dedicated, nonswitched data paths. But PVC-oriented frame relay is not optimal for the connectionless LAN environment, in which the use of switched virtual circuit (SVC) connections are preferred because such circuits provide network resources only when necessary. Vendors are already working to resolve this issue. More limiting are frame relay's data rates, which can not support voice or video. These will continue to be relegated to guaranteed-fixed-rate T1/ T3, or be satisfied by faster broadband networks. When these faster networks become available, frame relay will be relegated to slower traffic (much as X.25 is today) or serve as the access protocol into the faster networks.

9.5. ATM-BASED NETWORKS

9.5.1. LANs

LAN bandwidth continues to increase. Today FDDI pushes the bandwidth of LANs to 100 Mb/s, and fast Ethernet is on the horizon. However, upgrading shared-media LANs just delays the bandwidth congestion problems that are inherent in all shared LANs. The capacity of shared-media networks is only as large as the speed of the common bus. Bandwidth can not be added as needed. In contrast, ATM-based LANs allow users to connect to the network at their required speed, adding bandwidth as needed. ATM removes the limitations of shared LAN backbones by collapsing them into the ATM switching fabric.

The typical extended ATM LAN will employ an ATM switch to link slower LANs. To interconnect a series of LANs, multiple switches can be concatenated together (Figure 9.8). The switches will be more powerful than today's intelligent LAN hubs in terms of processing power, routing capability, and network management. Also, the ATM switch is distinguished from today's hubs in that its total bandwidth is the sum of the bandwidths of its input ports. Thus, with an ATM switch, information can travel from any port to any other port without being blocked. In contrast, traffic on bus-based hubs can be blocked if there are too many sources on the bus.

9.5.2. Public Broadband Networks

Future broadband public networks will blend cell relay switching and synchronous optical transmission, creating an ultrahigh-frequency switching fabric. A single multiservice platform will support POTS,

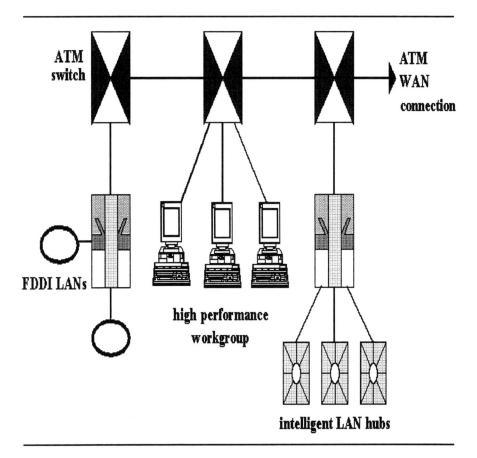

Figure 9.8. Concatenated ATM switches.

ISDN, frame relay, SMDS, and BISDN. Users will dynamically allocate bandwidth among a variety of services and redirect traffic between subnetworks. Voice communications, video exchanges, and supercomputer data will all be switched at the same time and as conveniently as data alone is today. The first ATM services will involve MANs, frame relay, and LAN interconnection. Public ATM networks are already emerging from trials and government sponsored research. Soon AT&T, GTE, MCI, Sprint, the RBOCs, and international PTTs in France, Germany, Japan, and other nations, will offer ATM switching services. New players are also getting involved as alternative access providers and system integrators use ATM to enter this lucrative market.

9.5.3. Telco/PTT

Many experts estimate that full ATM-based wide area networks from the public carriers will begin rolling out in 1994. Among the RBOCs currently field-trialing ATM switches is BellSouth Corporation, which linked a supercomputer in North Carolina to medical imaging equipment in another part of that state. Both Nynex and U.S. West also have trials underway. Among the independent carriers, GTE SPANet intends to provide a real-time gigabit-rate fusion of voice, video, and imagery. Meanwhile, Sprint is constructing an ATM network for the US Department of Energy and NASA. This network will operate at 45 Mb/s in 1993, 155 Mb/s in 1994, and 622 Mb/s in 1995. Sprint will offer commercial ATM service on a case-by-case basis starting in 1993, with a standardized pricing schedule in 1994. Sprint intends to add BISDN and SONET capabilities in early 1995 and will combine its private line and circuit-switching voice services with ATM-based services under the ATM backbone. Five European network operators are testing ATM technology across national boundaries: England's British Telecom International, Germany's Deutsche Bundespost Telekom, France's Telecom, Italy's ASST/STET, and Spain's Compania Telefonica Nacional de Espana.

These networks can transfer huge files—gigabytes heading toward terabytes—from one site to another. Once existing only in the realm of science fiction, these networks will flash information around the globe at the speed of light. The benefits will be astounding: hitherto insoluble problems in computing will be solved. The networks could be used for metacomputing in which remote mainframe computers can be tightly coupled in real-time for cooperative processing. Or they could significantly speed progress in modeling the global climate and human genetic research. Nonetheless, they are based on science fact, not fiction, and their greatest impact will be on satisfying the on-demand bandwidth needs created by daily business transactions.

9.5.4. Other Providers

The Federal Communications Commission's decision to allow competitive access providers to collocate their equipment in local exchange carrier's central offices has encouraged ATM networks from new competitors. MFS Datanet Inc. is building a nationwide fiber optic network supported by 13 ATM switches. The network will provide customers with high-speed LAN interconnection service (HLI) at native LAN speeds. HLI service includes long-distance transport, associated hardware and software support, and 24-hour monitoring and maintenance with a 90-

minute response time for service. Science Applications International Corp. (SAIC), a systems integration company, plans a less ambitious 45 Mb/s transmission service. SAIC will use WilTel Communications Systems Inc's nationwide fiber optic network and ATM switches to provide a nationwide switched broadband service providing high bandwidth for interLATA interconnection. Their network could be used to interconnect frame relay or SMDS, or it could transmit combinations of multimedia data. This is an opportunity that the cable television companies can ill-afford to miss. Time Warner, for example, intends to spend billions upgrading its network so that it can offer digitally stored movies on demand to cable television customers.

9.6. BISDN

While SMDS is a network service, BISDN is a service platform. A wide range of customer data, voice, and video applications is supported by a single BISDN network, using a limited set of network interfaces and network equipment configurations. BISDN takes advantage of the availability of high-capacity synchronous optical fiber networks (SONET/SDH) to transport enormous quantities of information reliably. Access to BISDN will be at 155 Mb/s and 622 Mb/s using high-speed, fixed-length ATM cells. With that much capacity, BISDN is expected to carry a multitude of services. While services supporting asynchronous data and voice will require only a portion of the bandwidth, others supporting imaging and LAN interconnection may use the entire channel.

With BISDN, private networks require only a small number of physical interfaces. Users requiring 45 Mb/s for high-quality videoconferencing, for example, could simply dial up a 45 Mb/s connection. Virtually any bandwidth between network locations could be established on demand. The list of services that could be provided with BISDN is just beginning to unfold. They fall into two basic categories: interactive and distributed. Interactive services will include videoconferencing, videotelephony, high-speed data, electronic mail with images, and interactive database services with high-resolution imaging and audio enhancements. Distributed services will include cable TV (existing quality), high-definition cable TV, pay-per-view TV, and compound document distribution.

9.7. NISDN

Deployment of ISDN has been slow. In 1991, a group consisting of regional Bell operating companies, switch vendors, computer manufacturers and large end-users committed to a revised Bellcore-driven technical standards known as National ISDN-1. The National ISDN-1 package is less comprehensive than the original ISDN Phase 1.1 Technical Reference. It represents a compromise between specifications developed by Bellcore and the North American ISDN Users' Forum. The purpose of the narrowband integrated services digital network (NISDN) is to accelerate deployment of ISDN services.

NISDN, now being deployed in some regions, is subdivided into basic rate interface (BRI) and primary rate interface (PRI). The BRI, also known as '2B+D', consists of two 64 kb/s B channels (DS0s) and one 16 kb/s D channel for common signaling and control. PRI or '23B+D' carries twenty-three 64 kb/s DS0 channels and one 64 kb/s D channel for common signaling and control. For NISDN, the SONET remote fiber terminal (RFT) may be more appropriate than an ADM. Its BRI ISDN interface would provide two DS0s for the 2B channels (64 kb/s), while the 16 kb/s D channel for signaling and control could share a fulltime DS0 with three other D channels in a 4:1 time division multiplexing arrangement. The primary rate service of '23B+D' or 24 DS-0s would be a full DS-1 interface mapping into floating VT1.5s of STS-1.

9.8.   CABLE TV NETWORKS

Cable TV networks in the United States are now being transformed into multiservice broadband networks. These networks are being built on optical fiber platforms and incorporate network redundancy available with SONET rings (Figure 9.9). This 'ring of rings' structure features signal redundancy at three levels: headend-to-headend, headend-to-hub, and hub-to-feeder.

- Applications Ring: The applications ring connects headends, local exchange carrier central offices, long-distance telephone carrier POPs, video-on-demand and multimedia playback centers. This resembles the new ring networks that link a local exchange carrier's serving offices with tandem offices and interexchange carriers. These rings operate at OC-3 or higher.
- Trunking Ring: Whenever a single headend location cannot serve all customers, a trunk ring that extends access distances to about 11 or 12 miles is used. The hubs on the trunk ring can be simple signal repeater locations fed by digital or amplitude modulated signals over fiber, or microwave receiving stations. Sometimes, hubs can add local off-air broadcast or satellite signals to the signal stream.
- Distribution Ring: The distribution ring carries telemetry data and upstream signals for interactive programming and services in the 5

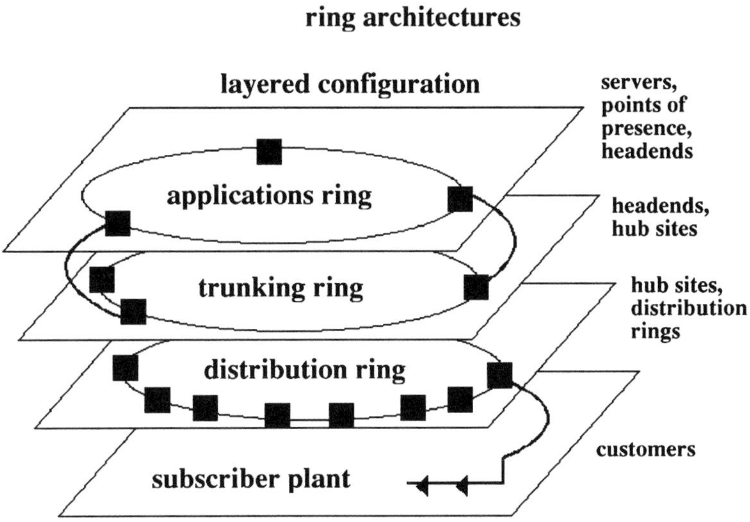

ring architectures

layered configuration

servers,
points of
presence,
headends

applications ring

headends,
hub sites

trunking ring

hub sites,
distribution
rings

distribution ring

subscriber plant

customers

Figure 9.9.   Cable TV networks.

to 30 MHz spectrum. The 54 to 550 MHz band could support 75 analog video channels. Bandwidth from 550 to 850 MHz could carry 500 channels of compressed digital video, and the 450 MHz between 850 MHz and 1.3 GHz would be reserved for telecommunications and personal communications services.

The deployment of this architecture based on SONET will be driven by the development of markets for new services such as video-on-demand and personal communications, as well as competition between the cable TV companies and LECs.

9.9.   CONCLUSION

Broadband Telco/PTT services are somewhat of a mystery—the clues are there, but the jury is out with regard to whether a particular service will succeed. The stakes for solving this mystery are high—nothing less than the competitive health of a given enterprise. The equipment to accomplish this task already exists in the guise of switches, hubs, multiplexers, and routers. Meanwhile, broadband networks are being built to work with existing networks, as backbones for private networks and as overlays for public networks. Services employing ATM, BISDN, cell, and frame relay are becoming available. The selection between them is predicated upon a clear understanding of what they can and can not do, and how they fit into the existing networks.

All the processing power of today's computers is relatively ineffective unless they can be interconnected efficiently within the office or on a global scale. Unfortunately, until standardized rates and tariffs are published, network managers will be forced to pick up clues and piece them together themselves. Only careful consideration will solve this mystery. For broadband communications is not just a matter of available equipment and services—it's a matter of planning.

10

Planning Considerations

10.1. INTRODUCTION

The fundamental changes taking place in telecommunications with regard to technology and business orientation are creating new business realities. No business is an island—all are interconnected by a vast global communications network. How effectively this network is used may very well determine whether a particular enterprise survives or dies.

The Telco/PTTs are making sophisticated broadband switching fabrics and services, as well as new methods of managing them, available to their customers. This evolving broadband public network will serve business and residential customers with equal facility. Business and residential customers will eventually use the same basic communications technologies for an array of bandwidth-hungry applications. Now is the time to plan, before the enterprise network reels under the impact of high-bandwidth applications—applications that have become as much a part of the desktop during the 1990s as personal computers did in the 1980s. Businesses need to devise ways to gain competitive advantage through the intelligent application of their telecommunications networks.

10.2. ASSESS THE SITUATION

Although the gap between LANs and WANs has narrowed, each has its own set of rules. The LAN is often considered a combination of cabling, hardware, and software, all used for connecting computers. Today, this view must be extended to include a spider's web of communications links, both within and between locations, that transports voice and data. Accommodating the bandwidth needs of advanced business transactions is crucial to taking advantage of this communications network. The infrastructure decisions for both public and private networks remain tied to the bandwidths demands of everyday business transactions.

Many managers are now faced with the task of figuring out when to finesse their networks by means of transitional approaches, and when to make the quantum leap. But the traditional sources for this information, computer hardware and software companies, may be just as much in the dark as individual managers. The questions are too varied. For example, while FDDI and frame relay are making progress, fast Ethernet and ATM are also advancing rapidly. Does it make sense to invest in temporary solutions when the right selection will bring true voice/data integration in the next decade? The anticipated progression of broadband technology from ATM LAN switching, to desktop applications, and finally to long-distance SONET/SDH networks, will change the networking equation (Figure 10.1).

10.3. MATCH NETWORKS TO BUSINESS NEEDS

Network managers need to keep an eye on costs, but should not lose sight of the future. Today's telecommunications network facilitates strategic business applications. The promises of broadband applications

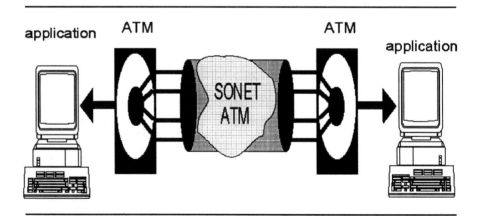

Figure 10.1.   Desktop-to-desktop broadband network.

have prompted many businesses to contemplate changes in their networks. Change begins with a complete analysis that matches needs and expectations to vendor and carrier offerings. The best place to jump in is at the LAN level. Begin by experimenting with products that provide high-speed transport and are crucial for high-bandwidth business applications, such as ATM.

In 1993, when products became available for the construction of ATM campus or office backbones, a number of progressive organizations installed ATM-based LANs to gain the economies and efficiencies of increased backbone network bandwidth. High-speed routers and bridges interconnected these LANs. These organizations will be ready for the second generation of routers, multiprocessor reduced instruction set computing (RISC) machines, supporting very high-speed routing. They will connect directly to the ATM infrastructure, providing a migration path to the desktop, where ATM will enable more sophisticated groupware, video, voice, and multimedia operations.

Finally, do not overlook the promise of ATM as a global area network strategy. Public and private network ATM use will ensure, for the first time, seamless end-to-end connectivity. Global use of ATM depends on the availability of fiber optic facilities. The rate at which SONET/SDH equipment is deployed within the Telco/PTT infrastructure will determine the rate at which high-speed, wide-area digital transport facilities become available. Fortunately, the groundwork for establishing critical mass is near completion.

10.4. UNIFY COMMUNICATIONS

A hybrid strategy, in which current data technologies co-exist with ATM and SONET/SDH, is a realistic approach. This will protect the installed investment, keeping the token ring, Ethernet and FDDI LANs intact, while ATM adapters are added in the hub or at the desktop.

10.4.1. Consider Carrier Services

Evaluating an enterprise-wide broadband network and comparing it with alternative networks gives a better sense of what broadband applications can and can not deliver. Broadband networks will create a host of exciting services, including:

* Business video conferences
* High-definition image transfer
* Distance learning

- Interactive TV
- Real-time manufacture and performance data reviews
- Ongoing market reports
- Medical diagnosis and consultation
- Working and shopping from home
- Video-on-demand entertainment
- Worldwide video telephone calls

When evaluating the effective cost of these services, there are several aspects to consider:

- *Fixed costs* are the one-time installation charges of circuits as well as equipment.
- *Periodic costs* are the recurring charges for leasing the circuits, and can vary greatly with distance and type of service and carrier.
- *Usage costs* are incurred each time the circuit is used and may be per minute, per packet, or per session.
- *Maintenance costs* are associated with equipment and network. For example, some frame relay carriers offer end-to-end service that includes routers on customers' premises.

The assessment should be based upon more than just cost. The coalescing of the communications and computer industries is accelerating switching and distribution capabilities. Those capabilities will provide the residential and business customer with powerful broadband services via the public switched network. The challenge facing businesses today is how to incorporate these services into on-demand networking solutions.

10.4.2. Unconnected Pockets of LANs

One migration strategy begins by speeding up LANs and providing switching capability. This strategy gives full bandwidth to each user and may be implemented with either available Ethernet switches or ATM. For many desktop users, 10 Mb/s remains adequate, and most hub vendors are working on some form of Ethernet switching. Nonetheless, Ethernet switches are only a step along the path to ATM. So wiring issues must be addressed today. If new wiring is being installed, or if existing wiring is being upgraded, make certain the cable plant can support ATM. A rule of thumb to employ is that on campus networks, fiber optic cable should be used; in buildings, use class 5 unshielded twisted-pair as a minimum standard.

Advancements in lasers, switching, and broadband standards will hasten deployment of ATM, the first communications technology equally at home in the LAN and the WAN. Today many major data communications manufacturers have announced ATM products. ATM-based LAN switches are available, and some private network installations of ATM are underway (Figure 10.2). For the first time, there is a logical way to integrate local- and wide-area communications. ATM defines an open, interoperable interface between networks, enabling users to take advantage of high-performance features and services. Initially, ATM will advance in organizations that want to deploy bandwidth-hungry applications in a LAN or campus environment. Campus network installations based on ATM will spur growth in the ATM interconnection market as ATM forms the basis for emerging broadband

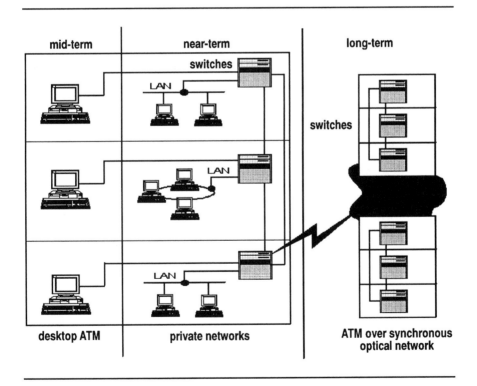

Figure 10.2.　ATM progression.

tariffed services over public networks. Within two years, a wide variety of ATM products will exist, including some from public network carriers. Frame relay and SMDS will be supported over ATM networks. The LAN-WAN barrier will begin to break down as similar transport protocols are used over both types of networks.

10.4.3. Global Ubiquity

The success of a networking technology is ultimately determined by its level of acceptance and its ability to solve user problems. The emerging high-speed networking technologies and services previously discussed are not globally available and will most likely change somewhat before they are universally accepted. When considering which technology to employ, users should understand how each fits into private and public networks, as well as whether it fits the access, transmission, or switching portions of the network. In the competitive race, all those portions will survive in *some* form.

It is anticipated that ATM will emerge as the switching technology, and SONET/SDH as the transport technology. Frame relay will be used as an access link to private and public networks. SMDS will provide the link to the public network for fiber LANs such as FDDI as well as lower-speed Ethernet and token ring LANs. The migration has already begun. For example, the expansion of existing fiber optic installations and improvements in the reliability of high-speed transmissions over copper will lead to widespread ATM installation in the public telephone network. Many of the Telco/PTTs are developing ATM networks that, in the future, will interconnect. This task is made possible by the existence of common standards for ATM in the U.S., Europe, and Asia.

Telco/PTTs will offer transport services to the general public that deliver advanced capability such as multiple channels of high-speed animation and data to the business market. Fortunately, network managers can make the necessary investments today to meet their imminent network challenges, while maintaining a clearly defined path. Consider the following:

- LANs and attached personal computers will continue to grab market share from earlier mainframe and minicomputer networks.
- X.25 still dominates data communications in terms of installed interfaces and actual use. However, frame relay is making in-roads into existing X.25 applications. Frame relay grew rapidly in the early 1990s into an international standard supported by many car-

riers and vendors, and is essentially the next generation of X.25 that uses high-grade digital lines to offer much greater speed.

- Both frame relay and ATM are suited to the access section of private and public networks. Frame relay addresses today's megabit transport and access. ATM addresses multimegabit transport and is suited for switching as well.
- ATM is the core technology for broadband ISDN services.
- SONET/SDH will become the dominant public network transport of the decade, first overlaying, then replacing, asynchronous networks.

10.5. MANAGEMENT STANDARDS

Although proprietary networks have dominated for decades, the 1980s witnessed the decline of their influence. Users needed access to the latest productivity-enhancing technology, no matter who the supplier was. Proprietary networks locked users out of the decision-making process, forcing them to depend on single vendors. The rise of the personal computer, LANs, and the standardization of the WAN has provided the opportunity for open, standard implementations. While true for equipment implementations, the network management of this equipment has been particularly difficult to standardize. This occurred because there are not one, but two open standard protocol suites: the OSI reference model discussed throughout this book, and the TCP/IP.

TCP/IP protocols are available, and OSI protocols, although more advanced, are not being developed fast enough to supplant them. For example, there was much discussion about the common management information services protocol (CMIP) of OSI replacing the simple network management protocol (SNMP) of TCP/IP. But the standard for CMIP was not accepted before the SNMP evolved, and SNMP II was released to fill many of the SNMP gaps, such as the security issues raised by the government and private industries. Originally developed to manage the routes on the Internet, SNMP now accommodates virtually any manageable network device. Since many vendors have written SNMP interfaces for their products, that protocol has become the most widely accepted standard for network management.

10.6. NEW ROLES

For leading edge corporations, networks are a permitting function, and the people concerned with their design and maintenance—from the support technician to the chief information officer—are the agents of change.

Today the corporate network can be a business unit expected to contribute to the bottom line, just like any other business unit. The user is a customer who should be treated just like any other customer. The information provided by the network is so important to the enterprise that networking people with management skills and knowledge are highly valued. What types of management skills and knowledge? The same as those used by other top executives, plus *an awareness of changing communications technology*: leadership, a strong sense of business practices, attention to the bottom line, an understanding of the corporate mission, and enough technological savvy to be the technology *expert* in the company (or at least the employ of staff members that can fill that role). The challenge is to develop the interpersonal communications required to sell new data networking technology. Leadership in this area will promote credibility and provide commensurate rewards.

10.7.   CONCLUSION

Underestimating the amount of traffic in the enterprise network, and the issues in getting it to remote locations, is not unusual in these, the early days of broadband LANs and WANs. Traditional network planners are not familiar with this environment. Fortunately, broadband networks are beginning to fulfill the promise of the information age. This revolution in data communications has provided a whole new generation of computer hardware and software applications that will be combined over broadband networks in ways that replace traditional computers, telephones, and televisions. The human and technological interfaces of multimedia communications have left the laboratory and entered the mainstream, making businesses more productive. Information can be organized to supply answers easily anywhere in the workgroup, the enterprise, and the world. This process of making information more accessible, understandable, and usable is bandwidth-intensive, providing further incentive for the rapid deployment of broadband networks.

Broadband Network Standards

A. NORTH AMERICAN STANDARDS

ATM Standards

T1S1.5/92-001:	AAL SSCOP baseline document
T1.ATM-199X:	ATM layer functionality and specification
T1.AL4-199X:	AAL 3/4 common part T1.CBR-199X AAL for constant bit rate services functionality and services
T1S1.5/92-005:	connectionless service layer functionality and services
T1S1.5/92-010:	AAL5 common part functionality and services
T1S1.5/92-111:	constant bit rate AAL architecture references (continued)

Bellcore—technical advisories and requirements for BOCs

ATM Standards

TA-NWT-001113:	asynchronous transfer mode (ATM) and ATM adaptation layer (AAL) protocols generic requirements

BISDN Standards

FA-NWT-001109:	broadband ISDN transport network elements framework generic criteria

FA-NWT-001110: broadband ISDN switching system framework generic criteria

FA-NWT-001111: broadband ISDN access signaling framework generic criteria for Class II equipment

TA-NWT-001112: broadband-ISDN used to network interface and network node interface physical layer generic criteria

SR-NWT-001763: preliminary report on broadband ISDN transfer protocols

SMDS Standards

TR-TSY-000772: generic requirements in support of switched multimegabit data service

TR-TSY-000773: local access switching system generic requirements in support of SMDS

SONET Standards

TR-TSY-000233: wideband and broadband digital cross-connect systems generic requirements and objectives

TA-TSY-000253: SONET transport systems: common generic criteria

TA-TSY-000303: IDLC system generic requirements, objectives and interface: feature set C—SONET interface

TR-TSY-000418: generic reliability assurance requirements for fiber optic transport systems

TA-TSY-000496: SONET ADM generic requirements

TR-TSY-000496: SONET add/drop multiplex equipment (SONET ADM) generic requirements and objectives

TR-TSY-000499: transport systems generic requirements (TSGR): common requirements

TA-TSY-000755: SONET fiber optic transmission systems requirements and objectives

TA-TSY-000773: local access system generic requirements, objectives and interface in support of SMDS

TR-TSY-000782: SONET digital switch trunk interface criteria

TA-TSY-000842: generic requirements for SONET-compatible digital radio

TA-TSY-000917: SONET regenerator generic requirements

TA-TSY-001042: generic requirements for operations interfaces using OSI tools: SONET transport

IEEE—802.X series of LAN standards

IEEE 802.3: Ethernet

IEEE 802.5: token ring

IEEE 802.6: distributed queue dual-bus subnetwork of a metropolitan area network

B. EUROPEAN STANDARDS

BISDN Standards

I.113: vocabulary of terms for broadband aspects of ISDN

I.121: broadband aspects of ISDN

I.150: B-ISDN asynchronous transfer mode functional characteristics

I.211: B-ISDN service aspects

I.311: B-ISDN general network aspects

I.321: B-ISDN protocol reference model and applications

I.327: B-ISDN functional architecture

I.361: B-ISDN ATM layer specification

I.362: B-ISDN ATM adaptation layer (AAL) functional description

I.363: B-ISDN ATM adaptation layer (AAL) specification

I.413: B-ISDN user-network interface

I.432: B-ISDN user-network interface—physical layer specification

I.610: OAM principles of the B-ISDN access

Appendix 2

Glossary

10BASE2 An 802.3 standard: 10 Mb/s transmission BASEband with 185 meters per thin (RG-58A/U) co-ax segment. Standard physical layer option for CSMA/CD.

10BASE5 An 802.3 standard: 10 Mb/s transmission BASEband with 500 meters per co-ax segment. Standard physical layer option for CSMA/CD.

10BASE-T An 802.3 standard: 10 Mb/s transmission BASEband over twisted-pair. Standard physical layer option for CSMA/CD.

AAL ATM Adaptation Layer: The ATM standards that specify the procedures to be followed to segment variable-length data packets into cells for transport through an ATM network, and then to reassemble as they exit the network. The AAL is subdivided into the SAR and the convergence sublayer.

ANSI American National Standards Institute: United States' representative to the CCITT.

ATM Asynchronous transfer mode: A form of fast-packet switching technology, using an asynchronous time division multiplexing technique: the multiplexed information flow is organized into fixed blocks called *cells*. It is 'asynchronous' in the sense that the recurrence of cells containing information from an individual user is not necessarily periodic.

Bandwidth A measure of information-carrying capacity.

BISDN Broadband ISDN. (See ISDN.)

Bridge A device that connects two or more LAN networks and forwards frames between them. Bridges can usually be made to filter frames, for example, to forward certain traffic only.

Broadcast A packet delivery system that delivers a copy of a given packet to all hosts that attach to it is said to 'broadcast' the packet.

CAD/CAM Computer-aided design/computer-aided manufacturing.

CCITT Comite Consulatif International Telegraphique et Telephonique, also known as the International Telegraph and Telephone Consultative Committee. A unit of the International Telecommunications Union (ITU) of the United Nations.

Cell A short, fixed-length packet used in the ATM high-speed packet switching technique, consisting of 53 bytes, 5 of header and 48 of payload.

Cell Relay See ATM.

CLP Cell Loss Priority: A cell header field that is used to provide guidance to the network in the event of congestion.

Connectionless Communication without a path for end-to-end connection being established first. Sometimes called *datagram*. A LAN would be an example.

Connection-oriented Communication proceeds through three well-defined phases: connection establishment, data transfer, and connection release. Examples are X.25, Internet TCP, OSI TP4, and ordinary telephone calls.

CPE Customer premises equipment: Generic name for transmission devices that are located in, and owned by, the public service customers.

CRC Cyclic redundancy check: An error detection scheme.

CSMA/CD Carrier sense multiple access with collision detection. A contended access method in which stations listen before transmission, send a packet, and then free the line for other stations. Also the access method used in Ethernet and IEEE 802.3.

CSU Channel service unit: A digital DCE unit for DDS lines.

Datagram An abbreviated, connectionless, single-packet message from one station to another.

DCE Data communications equipment, or data circuit-terminating equipment. In common usage, synonymous with *modem*: The equipment that provides the functions required to establish, maintain, and terminate a connection, as well as the signal conversion required for communications between the DTE and the telephone line or data circuit.

DMA Direct memory access: A fast method of moving data between two processor subsystems without processor intervention.

DQDB Distributed queue dual bus: IEEE 802.6-defined cell-relay standard for SMDS.

DSU Digital service unit: DCE common equipment used to connect a customer's DTE to public network facilities or to CSU-equipped DS1 facilities.

DTE Data terminal equipment: The equipment serving the network DCE as the data source, the data sink, or both.

EIA   Electronics Industry Association: A standards group within ANSI for the electronics industry.

Ethernet   An IEEE 802.3 LAN first developed by Xerox, then sponsored by DEC, Intel, and Xerox. An Ethernet LAN uses co-axial cables and CSMA/CD.

FDDI   Fiber distributed data interface: A high-speed networking standard. The underlying medium is fiber optics, and the topology is a dual-attached, counter-rotating token ring.

Flow control   Control of the rate at which hosts or gateways inject packets into a network or internet, usually to avoid congestion.

Frame   Variable length, addressed data unit identified by a label at layer 2 of the OSI reference model.

Frame relay   A networking packet delivery interface with an historical basis in X.25.

Gateway   A special-purpose, dedicated computer that attaches to two or more networks with different communications protocols and routes packets from one to the other.

GFC   Generic flow control: A cell header field used for multiplexing for access to an ATM network.

HEC   Header error control: A cell header CRC field that can be used to correct single-bit errors in the header and to detect multiple-bit errors.

Header   The bits within a cell allocated for functions required to transfer the cell payload within the network.

Internet   A collection of packet-switching networks interconnected by gateways with protocols that allow them to function logically as a single, large, virtual network. When written as **Internet**, the word refers specifically to the Defense Advanced Projects Research Agency (DARPA) Internet and the TCP/IP protocols.

IP   Internet Protocol. See TCP/IP.

ISDN   Integrated digital services network: ISDN combines voice and digital network services in a single medium, making it possible to offer customers digital data services as well as voice connections through a single 'wire.' The standards that define ISDN are specified by CCITT.

ISO   International standards organization: An international body that drafts, discusses, proposes, and specifies standards for network protocols. ISO is best known for its seven-layer reference model that describes the conceptual organization of protocols.

LAN   Local area network: A data communications network confined to a limited geographic area (up to six miles, or about 10 kilometers) with moderate to high data rates (100 Kb/s to 100 Mb/s). The area served may consist of a single building, a cluster of buildings, or a campus-type arrangement.

MAC   Media access control.

MAN   Metropolitan area network.

MAU   Medium access unit: A transceiver for 802.3 10BASE5 and 10BASE2.

Message   A complete transmission: Used as a synonym for a *packet* or *frame* of information, but often made up of several packets.

MIB   Management information base: A collection of objects that can be accessed via a network management protocol.

Multicast   A technique that allows copies of a single packet or cell to be passed to a selected subset of all possible destinations.

NISDN   Narrowband, or national ISDN.

NIC   Network interface controller: Circuitry, usually a PC expansion card, that connects a workstation to a network.

OSI   Open systems interconnection: Refers to a seven-layer hierarchical reference structure developed by the ISO for defining, specifying, and relating communications protocols. In the OSI model, suites of communications protocols are arranged in layers.

Packet   An information block identified by a label at layer 3 of the OSI reference model. It is the unit of data sent across a packet-switching network. See *frame* and *PDU*.

PCM   Pulse-code modulation: A modulation technique used to convert analog voice signals into digital form. Used for voice multiplexing on T1 circuits.

PDU   Protocol data unit: OSI terminology for *packet*. A PDU is a data object exchanged by protocol machines (entities) within a given layer. See *frame* and *packet*.

POTS   Plain old telephone service: Transported via PSTN, POTS offers traditional two-way voice conversation.

Protocol   A formal description of message formats and the rules two or more machines must follow to exchange those messages.

PSTN   Public switched telephone network.

PT   Payload type: A cell header field indicating the type of information in the cell payload.

PTT   Post, Telephone, and Telegraph Authority: The government agency that functions as the communications common carrier and administrator in many areas of the world.

PVC   Permanent virtual circuit: In a packet-switched network, a fixed virtual circuit between two users; no call setup or clearing procedures are necessary. Contrast with *SVC*.

Repeater   A hardware device that propagates electrical signals from one cable to another without making routing decisions or providing packet filtering. In OSI terminology, a repeater is a *physical layer intermediate system*. See *bridge*, *gateway*, and *router*.

Router A system responsible for making decisions about which of several paths network traffic will follow. To do this, it uses a routing protocol to gain information about the network, and algorithms to choose the best route based on predetermined criteria. In OSI terminology, a router is a *network layer intermediate system*. See *bridge, gateway*, and *repeater*.

SAR Segmentation and reassembly. One of two sublayers of the AAL with the functions of—on the transmitting side—the segmentation of higher layer-PDUs into a suitable size for the information field of the ATM cell and—on the receiving side—the reassembly of the particular information fields into higher layer PDUs.

SDH Synchronous digital hierarchy: Europe's version of SONET.

SMDS Switched multimegabit data service: A public packet-switching service proposed by Bellcore and offered by the telephone companies.

SNMP Simple network management protocol: The network management protocol of choice for TCP/IP-based internets.

SONET Synchronous optical NETwork: An advanced, fiber-based public network defined by a large family of related technical standards. See *SDH*.

STM Synchronous transfer mode: A transfer mode that offers, periodically to each connection, a fixed-length word. Contrast with *ATM*.

SVC Switched virtual circuit: In a packet-switched network, a temporary virtual circuit between two users. Contrast with *PVC*.

TCP/IP Transport control protocol/Internet protocol. TCP is the protocol that provides reliable, end-to-end stream transport. IP is the universal protocol of the Internet that defines the unit of transfer to be the IP datagram and provides the universal addressing scheme for hosts and gateways.

TDM Time division multiplexing: A technique used to multiplex multiple signals onto a single hardware transmission channel by allowing each signal to use the channel for a short time before going on to the next.

VCI Virtual channel identifier: A routing field in the header of a cell. Used to identify the virtual connection to which the cell belongs.

VPI Virtual path identifier: A routing field in the header of a cell.

WAN Wide area network.

X.25 X.25 is a CCITT standard for packet-switching that was approved in 1976. Its significance was that it standardized the structure of the packets and codified the functionality that could be embedded into them to facilitate networking.

About the Author

Robert P. Davidson, Ph.D. is president of Reference Point, a consultancy dedicated to data communications education and training. He is a Senior Member of the IEEE, has been named to the IEEE Computer Society List of Leaders, a member of the editorial board at *Spectrum* magazine, and past chairman of the International Test Conference. He is also the author of the KnowledgeBase™ series of multimedia personal trainers for the PC, and many landmark books in data communications, including:

- Internetworking LANs: Operation, Design and Management
- LANs to WANs: Network Management in the 1990s
- The Guide to Frame Relay and Fast Packet Networking
- The Guide to SONET: Planning, Installing & Maintaining Broadband Networks

Index